D1254835

# HAS THE
# CATHOLIC
# CHURCH
# GONE MAD?

*John Eppstein*

# HAS THE CATHOLIC CHURCH GONE MAD?

ARLINGTON HOUSE
New Rochelle, N.Y.

*Nihil obstat*

John M. T. Barton, S.T.D., C.S.S

Censor


*Imprimatur*

Victor Guazzelli, V.G.

Westminster, 3rd March 1971


The *Nihil obstat* and *Imprimatur* are official declarations that a book or pamphlet is free of doctrinal or moral error. No implication is contained therein that those who have granted the *Nihil obstat* and *Imprimatur* agree with the contents, opinions or statements expressed.

Library of Congress Catalog Card Number 71-179719


ISBN 0–87000–163–9


MANUFACTURED IN THE UNITED STATES OF AMERICA

# Contents

# Foreword

In this book I seek to analyse and assess, in the context of contemporary history, the changes and dissensions which have been at work within the Roman Catholic Church, since the Second Vatican Council opened the floodgates of controversy. I write as a layman who, beyond playing a fairly active part in parish and international life and devoting a special study to the Catholic tradition of international ethics, lays no claim to any particular theological or liturgical competence. Having devoted most of my life to editing and publishing information about many different nations, I have applied the criteria to which I am accustomed in an endeavour to determine, as objectively as possible, the real motives and relative strength of the various forces at work within the world-wide spiritual community to which I belong. The judgments which I have expressed will be shared by many, and disputed by many, of my co-religionists. They are based upon no position of neutrality or indifference, but on the standards of natural law, and of the supernatural faith which Pope Paul VI has reaffirmed in his 'Credo of the People of God', the chief target of the sneers and abuse of the modernist, anti-papal campaign, described in these pages. This *prise de position* does not, of course, dispense the contemporary historian from the duty of honest criticism of particular papal actions or policies; nor does it imply any blind opposition to change or reform.

This is not the only matter, though it is the main one, about which controversy rages. Where does one look for documentation? There is no lack of it on the side of the modernists who are promoting the notion of the new Conciliar Church. The agencies described in Part Four, aided by a kind of osmosis of progressives, have produced a quasi-unanimity of editorial policy and comment in the majority of the Catholic newspapers and reviews of the Western world and, what is more important, enjoy the support of highly-placed commentators in the main quality newspapers and in the mass media. Thus, with various degrees of popularisation, news and views on the following subjects enjoy most favoured treatment (a) sex, and in particular any defiance of Papal teaching or ecclesiastical discipline concerning matrimony, contraception, clerical celibacy etc; (b) attacks upon the Papacy and particularly the Roman Curia on the grounds of their supposed antipathy to collegiality or democracy; (c) emasculation of the articles of the Christian Faith especially in the new catechetical publications; (d) liturgical novelties; (e) any scandal or sensation concerning the abandonment of their vows by priests, monks or nuns; (f) ecumenical extravagances; and (g) Catholic support of Left-wing and especially anti-colonial policies. As will be seen from the text, we are indebted to *The Tablet* for some of the more alarming examples of these latter tendencies. Despite its own editorial slant, it also quite often prints letters, or even an article in a contrary sense, and records some papal utterances. It also reviews from time to time many of the new theological publications. Of the books supplying the philosophy of this movement Cardinal Suenens' *Coresponsibility in the Church*, which I review, is the most logical and coherent exposition of the notion of constructing the Church of the new era on a popular or democratic basis. Hans Kung's *The Church* (dedicated to the Archbishop of Canterbury) loosens its Roman bonds. The new Dutch *Catechism for Adults*, published in English – without episcopal sanction,* of course – has had a great influence in promoting the destruction of the traditional catechetical teaching. *Slant* was the

---

*A later edition, giving the Cardinals' criticisms in an appendix was sanctioned.

mouthpiece of the Catholic Marxists in England. I cite in the text or in footnotes some of the wilder French revolutionary sheets and organisations.

In view of the commitment of most of the better known Catholic publishing houses and periodicals to the modernist, progressive agitation, defenders of the papal position and of traditional Catholic doctrine and practices are necessarily thrown back upon more obscure publishers, and printed or multigraphed pamphlets. Some of these injure their cause by their expression of outraged feelings at the destruction of the old Latin Mass, or by their polemical style. There are others, such as Marcel Clément's *Homme Nouveau* in France or *Approaches* in England, which frequently contain texts which are valuable indications of the positions of both sides in the current theological and moral controversies†; where I have quoted any of them I have checked the sources and found them accurate. There are a number of more learned French Catholic articles critical of Teilhardism, as well as Jacques Maritain's notes on the subject in his latest book which I have found useful. Two organisations of English priests, who are averse to many of the new stunts and especially of the modern catechisms, issue bulletins, *Faith* and the more militant *Catholic Priests' Association*, while *Christian Order* and *The Keys* defend the now all but neglected Christian social doctrine.

For the English texts of papal allocutions or the more important acts of the Roman Congregations one can turn to the weekly English edition of the *Osservatore Romano* or multigraphed documents issued by the *Association of St. Peter* in Lancashire. The English versions of all the Pope's Encyclicals and of his *Credo* are published in pamphlet form by the *Catholic Truth Society*. Such are the published sources, very limited in circulation, and often difficult to come by, though valuable in quality, which can be set against the monstrous regiment of the mass media, mobilised in the service of the innovator or the rebel. As for substantial books, the old

---

†This refers particularly to material used in Part Four.

Catholic publishing firm of Desclée in France is one of the few who continue to produce solid works, including Cardinal Gabriel-Marie Garrone's *Que faut-il croire?*, which I have used extensively. Its English edition is published, not in Britain or the United States, but by Ecclesia Press in Ireland. Father Holloway's longer and more philosophical work on a similar theme *Catholicism: A New Synthesis* found, however, a new English publisher.

This short summary of some relevant publications and those which I mention in the text would have to be complemented with the titles of many others in different languages, which I have not been able to consult, in order to present a complete picture. But I believe it to be the case that there is a fantastic imbalance between the contemporary literature of Catholic orthodoxy, which is accessible, and the mass of printed matter, let alone television programmes, which favours the mania for religious change and particularly the sacrifice of traditional Christianity to the worship of that will-o'-the-wisp, Modern Man. This makes it all the more necessary to think things out for oneself and to form, as far as possible, an independent judgment upon how far this insane obsession may undermine the essential unity and stability of the Universal Church or whether – as I am inclined to believe – the old adage will once more prove true: *qui mange du Pape en meurt.*

John Eppstein
January 1971

# PART ONE

# Visible signs of disarray

# Chapter 1
# As seen from without

Has the Catholic Church gone mad? '*Non proprie dictu*', no doubt St. Thomas Aquinas would answer, '*sed secundum quid*'. Large numbers of Roman Catholics, and particularly highly vocal groups of friars, monks and secular clergy, even some bishops, undoubtedly say and do the craziest things, if judged by the standards of faith, morals and discipline which had hitherto been assumed to be fundamental characteristics of their Church. The Pope, however, and with him an indeterminate number of the silent faithful, whose loyalty to the Christian tradition does not enjoy the same limelight, evidently refuse, as we shall see, to abandon those foundations. Which of these two incompatible forces will win the day?

In the eyes of the intelligent observer the Roman Church, whether loved, criticised or opposed, seemed, before the confusion which followed the Second Vatican Council, to be the most solid and venerable pillar of civilisation. From it, or in reaction to it, all the other Christian communities, most of the laws and liberties, social and political institutions of the West, not excluding democracy and socialism, had historically derived and had found their way from Europe to the other Continents. But what distinguished it from all the Reformed Christian communities, which had broken away from it – and from one another – in the last four centuries, and indeed from the Eastern Churches, whose hierarchies enjoy the same Apostolic authenticity as the Roman episcopate claims, was its visible unity throughout the world under the undisputed authority of the Pope, as the Vicar of Christ and the successor of St. Peter. It was known for its firm defence of a single code of morality, as well as for the deposit of the Christian Faith, and, for all the shortcomings of its members, a singular tradition of sanctity, manifested generation after generation, as, in recent centuries, in St. Thomas More, St. Vincent de Paul, the Curé d'Ars, Dom Bosco or St. Theresa of Lisieux.

The most striking symbol of supranational unity was the Mass with its identical ceremonies and common Latin language. The celibate priesthood enshrined the ideal of unqualified devotion to Christ in the sacerdotal and pastoral ministry. The sanctity of the marriage bond was the main principle of sexual morality, just as the family, in the Church's doctrine, was the natural foundation of human society. The sacramental system involved not only the performance of visible or sensible signs as the vehicles of invisible grace but also the use of the material in the service of the spiritual. For this purpose were built and adorned all the old cathedrals and churches of Christendom; and the Sacrifice of the Mass inspired the noblest music of succeeding generations of composers.

Such were the distinctive contributions of the Roman Catholic Church to the culture of the world and the ideals which its members accepted. Some of other persuasions admired it and imitated its practices; others criticised it for failing to attain its ideals; others strongly opposed the papal authority; but it was respected.

It is difficult to find much evidence of that respect outside the Church today. In no more than eight years we have seen much to suggest that the Catholic Church is tearing itself to pieces. Every one of the essential tenets which we have outlined above has been called in question. We find the intolerant iconoclasm of younger priests emptying churches of every object of devotion all over Western Europe and the Americas; altars are stripped and replaced with plain communion tables. The exclusion of awe and mystery from the simplified congregational Eucharist deprives it of the quality which appealed most to Anglo-Catholics, and gave the Mass an appreciable affinity with the Eastern liturgies. The common liturgical language has disappeared in favour of tendentious vernacular paraphrases, not even translations. Papal authority is constantly attacked in the majority of professedly Catholic newspapers and publications of the Democratic countries, most of all when the Pope upholds traditional teaching on such matters of sexual morality as birth control, priestly chastity or divorce. The apostles of this defiance are almost always members of religious orders, including even the Society of Jesus, which was always believed to be distinguished by its loyalty to the Pope, but whose complete lack of discipline is now advertised to the world. The powers of Bishops, now organised in national conferences, are invoked against him, the Netherlands Espicopate's support of its 'Pastoral Council' in its attack on the celibacy of priests being so far the most flagrant example. Maximum publicity is given to religious and secular clerics who leave the priesthood to marry. There is unrestricted speculation, also widely publicised, by theologians who do not hesitate to call in question the most sacred objects of belief such as the divinity of Christ, the Virgin Birth, the miracles of the New Testament, the Resurrection and the Presence of Christ in the Eucharist. The same scepticism invades the seminaries, even the Gregorian University in Rome. Vocations for the priesthood are dwindling. And all this within a few years of a General Ecumenical Council which was to bring about a vast renewal of Christianity.

What has probably reduced respect for the Church more than anything is the impression that many of its leaders are leaning over backwards to persuade Protestants, not to speak of Humanists and Communists, that the Catholic Church is not the Church that it has always claimed to be. Indeed attempts to attenuate its authority and doctrines may well defeat the very ecumenical purpose that they are intended to serve. Nor can it be said that the recent emphasis placed on the social and economic duties of Catholics, especially since the Pope's Encyclical *Progressio Populorum*, rather than upon the spiritual life, has enhanced the quality of Catholicism. For good or ill, it has certainly given the Church in many countries a leftward lurch.

These are some of the obvious reflections upon the present unbalanced state of the Catholic Church which are most commonly made by serious non-Catholic observers.

It is only fair to record, however, that the disruptive phenomena described above are chiefly to be seen in Western and Southern Europe and among peoples of European origin in North and South America and Australia. The oppressed clergy and faithful of the Communist-ruled countries of Eastern Europe seem less disturbed. Nor is there any evidence that the Church has gone mad in Africa. On the contrary one reads, for instance, of 14,000 conversions in a single diocese of Tanzania, Mwanzi, in one year; more than the highest number recorded in any year in England and Wales, before the recent confusion practically put an end to them. These distinctions must be borne in mind in assessing the extent of the contemporary Catholic aberrations.

# Chapter 2
# As seen from within

All the aspects of disorder which the detached observer sees in the Catholic Church today have, of course, a sharper impact upon the practising Catholic since they impinge upon his intimate spiritual life.

It is the changes in the Mass and in the visible accompaniments of worship which hit the ordinary Catholic first and most painfully. That is how he and his family normally come into contact with the Church, whereas it is chiefly the intellectual minority which is moved one way or another by the controversial innovations of theologians and publicists, of which we shall have more to say later; and the scandal of monks and priests abandoning their vows is fortunately more often something read about than directly observed.

We shall outline in Part Three the actual changes in the liturgy effected between 1963-70 and apparently finalised by Pope Paul VI in his Apostolic Constitution of April 1969. But it is important to remember that, apart from the latitude allowed to Bishops of various countries, there have been two agencies of change at work. One is the alteration of public worship officially authorised by stages. The other consists in the semi-official directives and advices about the 'Liturgical Renewal' emanating at intervals from members of the Liturgical Consilium in Rome, in which debate continued for nearly five years and which was throughout the headquarters of the 'reforming' lobby. The most radical and often quite unauthorised interpretations have been placed upon the latter by enthusiasts. It is these which have caused most shock and scandal, especially in countries such as Belgium and Chile, where the hierarchy gave them free rein even while the Vatican Council was still sitting. There was in fact no general demand anywhere for the abandonment of the Latin liturgy or the destruction of the familiar ornaments of worship; and many of the faithful were horrified to see not only crucifixes, statues of the saints and altar candlesticks, but also chalices, pyxes and sacred vestments, sanctified by long use in their parish churches, on sale in the flea market in Brussels or the antique shops of Paris or Santiago. Good lay folk clubbed together to buy them back, to save them from that they considered sacrilege.

And who committed the sacrilege? In every case priests, and especially the members of religious orders who, as in the last Reformation four centuries ago, have taken the lead in the destruction of the beautiful and the repudiation of the traditional. Hubris and intolerance are, alas, the invariable characteristics of religious reformers, and none is more insensitive to the feelings of his co-religionists than the poacher turned game-keeper of today.

Let us take, since it is the most important point of the Catholic liturgy, belief in the real presence of Christ in the Blessed Sacrament. Here Rome seems to the bewildered believer to speak with two voices. On the one hand Pope Paul VI in his Encyclical *Mysterium Fidei*[1] writes,

> 'Liturgical laws prescribe that the Blessed Sacrament be kept in churches with the greatest honour and in the most distinguished position. It is not only while the sacrifice is being offered, the sacrament constituted, that Christ is truly Emmanuel, "God with us". He is so after the offering of the sacrifice . . . as long as the Eucharist is kept in churches and oratories'. And he speaks of the reserved sacrament 'as the spiritual centre of the religious community and the parish community'.

Again in the outspoken *Credo of the People of God* which he pronounced on the Feast of S.S. Peter and Paul in 1968 to

---

[1] 3 September 1965.

conclude the commemoration of the nineteenth century of the martyrdom of those Apostles, he speaks of the tabernacle, in which the Blessed Sacrament is reserved, as 'the living heart of our churches'.

On the other hand we are told of advices emanating from the Liturgical Consilium in Rome which avant-garde bishops and clergy have seized upon to justify the removal of the tabernacle from the high altar or even a special chapel to an obscure corner of the church, a hole in the wall or the crypt, for the deliberate purpose of discouraging attention to it. What is one to believe?

Cardinal Gabriel Garrone, Prefect of the Congregation for Catholic Teaching, in his profoundly spiritual book *This we believe*[2] speaks of

> ' all those men and women for whom going into a church means finding our Lord sacramentally. Who can measure the faith the Eucharistic presence has awakened, the love it has nurtured and the fidelity it has sustained? One cannot think without grief and anxiety of the vast decline in the potential for prayer that results from waning devotion to the Eucharist. The church that has been abruptly transformed into a kind of lifeless temple, where one has difficulty in finding the providential sign of our Lord and Saviour's presence, will soon be deserted'.

It is only too easy to find nowadays, in one country after another, a church which, thanks usually to the arbitrary tyranny of a progressive priest, has been turned into a 'lifeless temple', an abomination of desolation. It is uncongenial enough for those accustomed to the reverence of Catholic worship to have to put up with Mass celebrated at a bare table facing the people in a new church which is little more than an empty box. It is even more an outrage to their feelings to find their old and beautiful church stripped and desecrated. The tourist to Portugal for instance is adjured in his guide-book to admire the golden retables, the polychrome statues, the rich ornaments of the altars which

[2]*Shannon Press* 1969, translated from the French *Que faut-il croire?*, Desclée 1967 and published with an introduction by Cardinal John Wright.

adorn the Baroque churches of the 17th and 18th centuries all over the country. But if he goes, shall we say, to the parish church at Cascais – to mention a resort known to thousands of visitors – he will find a typical small Portuguese church of this kind, which only a year or two ago had its three altars – over-decorated no doubt – always alive with flowers, stripped to the bone. Everything which could be removed has gone, every statue, every picture, even the crucifixes and candles from the altars. A plain communion table with a white cloth, two stubby candles and a microphone dominates the scene on a platform in front of the denuded sanctuary; and there are no more flowers.

Yet one can find in the same country, as in many English Roman Catholic parishes still, churches retaining their familiar high altars and tabernacles and the flickering of votive candles. It all depends on the priest and the attitude of his bishop and nothing is more disturbing to the laity than to find that, with the liberties allowed to the clergy and the variety of new and incomplete service books, they are absolutely at the mercy of the local priests. The result is much confusion and cynicism. To quote Cardinal Garrone again,

> 'The Catholic faithful are justified in being worried, in protesting – we only wish they would protest more loudly as is their layman's right – when they see a minister take unscrupulous liberties with the sacraments and set himself up as the arbiter of the signs of faith. For in such instances, faith itself senses that it is threatened and rebels against sinful imprudences. If the sacraments of faith are abandoned to the arbitrary whims of any minister, they run the risk of no longer being the sacraments of faith. As a result, the believer who refuses to submit to the law of one man's private judgment may gradually turn away from a sacramental world that has lost all value in his eyes'.

Apart from the distress caused to devout Catholics by the iconoclasm and experimental aberrations which Cardinal Garrone describes, what are the reactions of the practising

Faithful as a whole to the new Mass? It is extremely difficult to generalise about conditions in different countries and continents: the present writer can only claim personal experience of the liturgical innovations in seven countries of Europe and North America and one in West Africa. From this and much published material one can offer the following estimate.

All Catholic congregations have clearly been divided into three parts, the relative importance of which varies from parish to parish. First, the majority, who are not intellectuals or internationally minded, soon became reconciled to the use of their ordinary language in the liturgy and take fairly readily to the collective participation, which is the order of the day, as do most priests, out of obedience, whether they like it or not. The children soon became used to it. After all, one either goes to Mass with one's family as a matter of weekly habit, or one does not. I know of no evidence of non-practising Catholics being won back to church; but those who are accustomed to go regularly are chiefly interested in the essential purpose of the Eucharistic Sacrifice, which is the Consecration and Holy Communion. Most of them realise that there is nothing they can do about the performance of the clergy, queer as it may seem, and eventually they become accustomed to any practice imposed by authority which does not affect the essential.

The second group are those cultured people who up till now have furnished the main intelligent support for the Catholic cause but now find themselves spurned by the Papacy; they are by no means only the aged or the well-to-do. These radical changes have taken the heart out of them. In common with boys and girls of all classes educated in many Catholic schools before the recent upheaval, they had learnt to know and love their missals, usually printed with the Latin and vernacular side by side, and, particularly where the Latin dialogue Mass had become the rule, understood the meaning of what they said or sung. For them and most of all for those who had left a national church to join, as they believed, the one supra-national Church, the loss of the Latin, which symbolized that unity and made them feel at home in any Catholic church in the world, is almost intolerable. Hence the formation of *Una Voce* and Latin Mass Societies striving to keep alive, in the face of a barely interested, or even hostile, episcopate, the continued celebration in Latin which the Vatican Council's Liturgical Constitution allows and indeed prescribed. They are mainly people of a certain age; but the branch in Chile, starting with a bare dozen members, at a time when the vernacular had been arbitrarily imposed in all churches, has become many hundreds strong, consisting entirely of undergraduates and young graduates of the University of Santiago, and has now raised a sufficient endowment to build a church of its own in which, with episcopal consent, Mass is exclusively sung in Latin. The more responsible of such bodies, accepting their obligations to Papal authority, adapt themselves to the Latin celebration of the New Order of the Mass. Others however are in danger of forming a 'schism of the Right', especially in the United States.

A great number of devout people both among the old European Catholic communities and among the younger dioceses of the Church in Africa have been deeply distressed by the apparently purposeless suppression of the familiar words which meant so much to them. An Anglican writer, Rosemary Sissons[3], has eloquently expressed the miserable confusion of the ordinary church-goer because of the novel departures from the beloved words of the Prayer Book in the Church of England. She might well be speaking for her Roman Catholic colleagues, who suffer from a similar scrapping of their familiar missals.

> 'All around me were other baffled worshippers, fumbling their way through little blue books and peering at pencilled instructions "kneel", "sit", "stand" – instructions which seemed to bear little or no relation to any spiritual inclinations on the part of the congregation'.

[3]In an article *Bread of Faith* published in the *Daily Telegraph Magazine*, 27 March 1970.

She goes on to complain of the effect of the experimental services which the Archbishops have introduced,

> 'For at least eight years we shall always be encumbered by leaflets and booklets, we shall never be free to pass through the well-known words to newness of worship. From week to week, we shall be constantly startled and irritated by lessons in unexpected places, by distorted prayers, truncated creeds, unfamiliar responses, strange rituals, and every Anglican visitor to another church will find himself an alien'.

It is true that the *Missa Normativa*, authorised by Pope Paul in April 1969 and now generally in use, while itself confirming the abolition of many venerable prayers and introducing a completely new lectionary, is intended to put an end to the wilder experiments which have caused so much scandal. But the new Ordo itself contains a number of alternatives and it has been brought into force long before any complete missals could be made available to priests or people. The bewildering regime of little bits of paper will be with us for years.

It is, of course, not only the matter of language and, what is more important, the omission from the new truncated service of certain elements to which, as we shall see below, the Tridentine Mass gave prominence, that worries so many of the faithful. It is the transformation of the priest, offering prayer and sacrifice to God at the altar on behalf of the people, into the caricature of a Protestant Minister shouting at them from the other side of a table or a reading desk, and the deliberate attack of the new instructions upon the practice of kneeling in prayer and other familiar gestures of devotion. A curious cult of the chair has been introduced. The priest (he is described as 'the president' in the general rubric of the new Mass) sits brooding at the congregation like a Buddha, when not reading the scriptures to them or addressing them himself. And the practical effect of his directing all prayers *at* them, whether from his desk or from the other side of the altar table, in the vulgar tongue, induces

13

a rhetorical tone, in which, while nominally addressing Almighty God, he is more engaged upon impressing his human hearers with his eloquence. Hence the people cannot avoid reactions to the personality of the minister, warts and all. This is far removed from the impersonal respect for the sacerdotal office, which has hitherto distinguished Catholic worship from that of the more congregational Protestant services and reduced individual distraction to a minimum. The use of the old hieratic language and exact rubrics governing the priest's actions helped to prevent personal defects from impinging upon the sacred office.

Nothing could be in more flagrant contrast to the tradition of the sacrificing priest than the following conception of the celebrant's task expressed in *Style and Presence in Celebration* by the Revd. R. W. Houda, a leading light of the International Committee on English in the Liturgy, whose loose and ugly texts are now inflicted upon Catholics who have the misfortune to live in English-speaking countries.

> 'Good presidency means an effort to solicit the attention of each person in the assembly with one's eyes as well as with one's general demeanour – to attend to anything else – book, bread, without attending to the persons present is the opposite to the style we seek'.

In other words the president (whom we have hitherto called the priest) is for all intents and purposes the political commissar dominating the proletariat.

The emphasis, clearly right in itself, upon the social character of the Eucharist seems to have been pushed to such an extreme, that the fact that each man, woman or child in church is an individual and distinct soul – each 'a spiritual universe' as Jacques Maritain says – is quite forgotten. For the Christian, as this writer has pointed out in discussing the changes[4], is not only a *member* of the Mystical Body in whose corporate worship he participates, but also a *person* whose response to and reception of grace can only be

---

'In *Le Paysan de la Garonne*. Des c le de Brouwer 1966.

individual. It is the disregard of this by the constant noise, the injunctions to stand, sit and repeat phrases in common which has made the new liturgy so distasteful. Nothing is missed more than the silence during the Canon of the Mass, broken only by the little bell rung at the supreme moment of Consecration and Elevation, in which one could almost feel the spiritual concentration of a great congregation.

The third section of the community, which except in the Netherlands and certain parts of the United States, seems to be numerically the smallest of the three, is that which is enthusiastic for the innovations and ready for the maximum of change. They welcome the attempted adaptation of the Catholic Church to the modern world for exactly the reasons for which the devout and more conservative distrust it. History means nothing to them, Latin is something alien and unknown. Freedom and democracy are more welcome than anything that savours of authority. Supernatural mystery has no place in the idiom of their daily lives, and the more the Church conforms to the social egalitarianism which is the prevailing climate of their political world, the more it seems to respond to their wishes. The nationalisation both of the liturgy and the episcopate is welcome, without any concern for the visible, supranational unity of the church, since they have no personal experience of other countries.

It is among this keen and vocal section of the Christian community that are to be found the minority, who not merely conform to the new liturgy – as do of necessity the bulk of practising Catholics – but are keen to take a hand in transforming the Church into something different. Like the 'world builders' of progressive politics, they are to the fore in any of the new committees or commissions or pastoral councils which give the laity a means of influencing ecclesiastical policy or directing Catholic activity in the social field. There is no doubting their fervour, just as no one questions the sincerity of the busy extremists, including the Communists, who secure control of English Trade Unions, since 90 % of the members cannot find time to attend the meetings.

While there is no reason beyond the habitual conformity of non-conformity to account for the fact, it is almost invariably those who are most in favour of the ugly ritual of the new puritanism, embellished if possible with pop music, who also support any public criticism of papal judgments, most of all in the matter of contraception; echo the ideas of those who demand the democratisation of Church authority; repeat the shibboleths of neo-modernist theology, and are caught up (through 'dialogue' with Communists) in the movement to turn the social action of Catholics into a revolutionary channel. We study in a later chapter the international propaganda organization for which these people are in any country the ready-made cannon-fodder. One is struck by the small number of names, whether of avant-garde clergy or laymen, which crop up again and again in the reports of any of these activities.

It is rare to find parochial life seriously disturbed as yet in England by the clash between this aggressive element and the traditional majority, though some nasty intrigues against conscientious parish priests can be recorded. Real danger to the faith is done by the capture of catechetical institutes and publications by modernist clergy. It is different in other parts of the world. In Latin American countries, where the structure of society is full of extreme inequalities, it is inevitable that the Christian social reformer should be drawn nearer to the Marxist revolutionary. The result is an acute division of the Catholic community into traditionalists and progressives with great embarrassment to the hierarchy.

In France, where conflicting ideas always become the flags of battle, groups of extremists of the Left made a concentrated effort in May 1968 to secure control of a number of large parishes in Paris by involving the parish priests in public debates and discussion in the churches, with a view to turning them into popular 'assemblies'. This was a by-product of the revolt in the Universities and was largely the work of a body calling itself *Bible and Revolution* organised by the Dominican Communist, Father

Blanquert, who took possession of the Centre of St. Yves, used by the Catholic students of the Faculty of Law. There was public brawling by these young revolutionaries during Mass in several large churches such as St. Séverin and St. Honoré d'Heylau. Avant-garde priests, had, of course, sold the pass. There was vigorous reaction by the bulk of the faithful to these interruptions and, not unnaturally, as the campaign developed, it was identified by its opponents with the intemperate advocacy of class warfare made in the preceding Lent by such people as Father Cardonnel[5]. There were counter-attacks by infuriated youths attached to the old religion, immediately described as Fascists, of course. They, for instance, pelted the avant-garde preacher Father Oraison as he entered the Church at Passy, and proceeded to sing the Credo loudly in Latin. How far this deplorable kind of war has spread to the rest of France it is difficult to determine, but what we have said is a good example of the dementia provoked both by the liturgical revolution and the accompanying theological and philosophical subversion. The resulting quarrels bring the Church into the thick of political controversy.

In Belgium this controversy is primarily linguistic, the struggle for ascendancy between Flemish and French. In the old days the feud was real enough, especially during the rise of the Flemish movement (whose leaders were my friends) at the end of the first World War. But, though priests were involved on both sides, the Latin Mass was the accepted bond of unity everywhere. The wholesale introduction of the vernacular by the Belgian Bishops immediately started the fight in every border parish, as well as in Brussels, where the French and Flemish-speaking populations are mixed, and in the coastal resorts to which people flock from all over the country in summer. The linguistic war in church services, as well as in teaching, immensely embittered the quarrel

---

[5]"I have no hesitation in saying it; the only Lent in which I believe would be that of a general strike which would paralyse a society founded on profit". Témoignage Chrétian

between Flemings and Wallons in the Catholic University of Louvain, and the Primate, Cardinal Suenens, and his fellow Bishops were powerless to prevent the splitting of the University into two separate parts, geographically distinct. It is a tragedy for Christendom.

Contrast this capitulation to linguistic nationalism in Europe with the position of the African Archbishop of Dakar in Senegal, whose diocesans are made up of various tribes as well as the resident French minority.

> 'The complete suppression of Latin in our Church services would be utter folly. The majority of the people do not understand French. Some of them can only participate in the celebration of the Mass through the medium of the Latin chants they have learnt. When a Mass is celebrated in the Cathedral in the Woloff language, three-quarters of the people do not understand it. On the other hand they know that the Gloria is a hymn of joy and adoration which gives them the feeling that they are all united in celebrating the Mass'.[6]

There are, it appears, many other parts of Africa where Latin remains as the bond of unity – and intellibigility – in Catholic worship. As a basic language it is even easier for many Africans to learn than the former colonial languages, English and French. A report from Ghana reads,

> 'Fortunately, here at Tarkwa, the Mass remains largely unchanged as yet, and it would be difficult to know, in fact, in what tongue it could be celebrated satisfactorily, when the languages, hereabouts comprise English, Ewe, Turi, Ga, Dagarti, Hausa and Ibo amongst others'.[7]

And Sir John Whyatt Q.C., an inveterate traveller, recording an experience in Tanzania, writes,

> 'Perhaps the most remarkable experience of all was when I was attending midnight Mass at a mission church on the slopes of Kilimanjaro and heard 3,000 Africans singing the Credo lustily in Latin'.[7]

Such testimony can only prompt the reflection that liturgical reforms, dictated, as they have been, by the pressure of

---

[6]Interview in *Paris-Match*, 22 February 1969.
[7]Quoted in *Lingua Sancta* published by the Latin Mass Society.

Americanism and European nationalisms, are a doubtful contribution to the good of the universal Church. On the other hand, there is evidence from African and Asian missions of the value of adapting Catholic rites to genuinely indigenous customs and using the traditional language of a homogeneous community. The case for a Chinese liturgy was already a venerable one.

What of the future? We have recorded very diverse reactions to the dislocation of the old liturgy and the substitution of the new forms of worship. While one can find no sign of enthusiasm, lay or clerical, for the latter, except from progressive political minorities of European extraction, they will in most places be carried out in loyalty to the Pope, even if *contre coeur*, and it is likely that for those who continue to go to church, habit will re-assert itself. One can point to no spiritual gain to compensate for the distress and confusion caused to the best of Catholics by avant-garde priests and their de-sacralised churches. On the other hand, where parish life is already healthy, with clergy who uphold the unchanging tradition of doctrine and sacramental life, attendance at Mass and the number of Communions remain at a high level, without changes in posture and wording having the slightest effect. 'Why does it matter?' is a question often heard from practising Catholics, who cannot see either the case for destroying what is familiar or the importance of particular innovations. *Vis inertiae* is sometimes a wonderful blessing. In other words these parishes are living on their pre-Conciliar capital. The real test will come when the old and trusted parish priest dies or retires and is replaced by a product of the seminaries or novitiates which, in many parts of Europe and North America at least, are riddled with modernism, politics and loose discipline, not to speak of the decline of vocations. Cardinal Garrone and his Congregation of Catholic Teaching have indeed a formidable task of restoration before them.

# PART TWO

# The second Vatican Council

# Chapter 3

# The Constitution on the Church

It is essential to any attempt to analyse the existing disorder in the Catholic Church to have a fair picture of what the Vatican Council was and did.

This congress of the whole Roman Catholic Episcopate, which observer-delegates from the majority of other Christian Churches also attended by invitation, was announced by Pope John XXIII in January 1959. It opened in October 1962 and closed after four sessions in December 1965. It was the 21st General Council of the Catholic Church (the 1st Council of Nicaea of AD 325 being reckoned as the first) and was originally intended to complete the work of the 1st Vatican Council, which was cut short by the invasion of the Papal States by the Piedmontese army in 1870. The old Pope's personal desire, however, was to bring the Church as a whole up to date; and, as this *aggiornamento* or programme of renewal was widely welcomed, most of all, of course, by the various groups who desired change, the agenda expanded, both in the prepatarory period and even more during the Council's own discussions, into a vast panorama which involved every aspect of morals, faith, discipline, worship, civics, and ecclesiastical organisation.

The result, excluding nearly a thousand footnotes of scriptural, patristic, papal and conciliar references, is a volume of over 103,000 words. It consists of two Dogmatic Constitutions, one on the Church, the other on Divine Revelation; a Constitution on the Sacred Liturgy and a Pastoral Constitution on the Church in the Modern World;

nine Decrees and three Declarations, all promulgated by Pope Paul VI 'Servant of the Servants of God, together with the Fathers of the Sacred Council, for Everlasting Memory'. The Decrees are on the Instruments of Social Communication (meaning the mass media), an unimpressive document; Ecumenism; the Eastern Uniate Churches; the Bishops' Pastoral Office in the Church; Priestly Formation; the Appropriate Renewal of the Religious Life; the Apostolate of the Laity; the Ministry and Life of Priests; and Missionary Activity. The Declarations are on Christian Education; on Relations with non-Christian Religions and on Religious Freedom. The relative importance of these different kinds of documents is not clear, but obviously the two Dogmatic Constitutions, are the most fundamental. All the more detailed observations contained in the later Decrees on bishops, priests, religious, laity and the missions are, for instance, implicit in the Constitution on the Church. For this reason and most of all because it seeks to complete the 1st Vatican Council's definition of the Papal office with the attributions of the episcopate, all the other parts of the Christian community and their mutual relationships, it has been hailed as the distinctive product of this particular Council. On the other hand it is the action arising from the Constitution on the Liturgy which, as we have seen, has had the most immediate impact upon the bulk of the Faithful.

## A general appreciation

It is a tragedy that the Council should have been followed (whether *post hoc* or *propter hoc* is a matter of acute controversy) by the sorry disarray of the Catholic community which we are studying in this book. The Conciliar documents as a whole reveal a deep spirituality, great scholarship, an abounding charity and the reverse of that exclusiveness and superiority with which the Roman Catholic Church has been so often reproached in the past. The drafting and editing of texts, which had to take account of all those trends in the thoughts of 2,800 Fathers which could be conciliated (often to the annoyance of progressives such as Cardinal Suenens), was a masterpiece of secretarial organisation, which must be the admiration of all of us who have experience of running international conferences. Archbishop, now Cardinal, Pericle Felici, the Secretary General, deserves the chief credit for this.

At the same time the Council, being human, was evidently not entirely exempt from the invariable rule of large international assemblies, *'toujours plus à gauche'*; not, of course, in the crude political sense, but in the sense that any pressure groups who were enthusiastic for change or for the adoption of their particular nostrums tended to win over or wear down sooner or later, with the necessary trimming, the central mass of members who had come, as did probably the majority of Bishops at the start, with no particular proposals of their own. This is especially discernible in the Constitution on the Liturgy, the first substantial text to be presented, before the majority of the Fathers were really used to the debate in Latin, which had been carefully put together by a keen minority of liturgical 'reformers' in advance. It can be seen also in the variety of social concepts and formulas, some very arguable, the references to the United Nations and the generalisations about modern man and the modern world, beloved of French sociologists, which found their way into that long rambling essay on the Church and the Modern World (*Gaudium et Spes*). This takes up nearly a quarter of the whole output of the Council and seems to contain all the points which could not be got in anywhere else. We shall refer to this later.

It is impossible in a short space to do justice to the Council documents as a whole. The pity of it is that they form so large a volume that only relatively few people can have the time or aptitude to read them all.[8] We shall be obliged

---

[8] They are, however, easily available in English. *Documents of Vatican II*, edited by Walter M. Abbott, S.J., published by Geoffrey Chapman, London and Dublin 1966.

THE SECOND VATICAN COUNCIL

therefore to concentrate on those passages, which have
given rise to subsequent controversy or which have introduced new elements into the Church's message.

## The Constitution on the Church

This has been described as the first full conciliar exposition
in history of the doctrine of the Church as a whole. After an
introductory chapter on the Mystery of the Church, a long
chapter defines it as consisting of the 'new People of God'
succeeding to the chosen people of the Old Testament.

> 'So it is that this messianic people, although it does not
> include all men and may more than once look like a small
> flock, is nonetheless a lasting and sure seed of unity, hope
> and salvation for the whole human race. Established by
> Christ as a fellowship of life, charity and truth, it is also
> used by Him as an instrument for the redemption of all'.

Baptism consecrates human beings as members of God's
people, the Church; other Sacraments – Confirmation, the
Eucharist and Penance – sustain them; Holy Matrimony
produces new citizens of human society. 'By the grace of
the Holy Spirit received in baptism they are made children
of God, thus perpetuating the People of God through the
centuries'.

The chapter then distinguishes the Catholic Faithful, who
accept the entire system of the Church and 'through union
with her visible structure are joined to Christ who rules
her through the Supreme Pontiff and the bishops', and other
baptised Christians 'who do not preserve unity of communion
with the successor of Peter', but who 'in some real way are
joined with us in the Holy Spirit' . . . 'In all Christ's disciples
the Spirit arouses the desire to be peacefully united in the
manner determined by Christ as one flock under one shepherd'. (Does it?) All this is very different from the attitude
of former Councils to those who were called heretics or
schismatics. The solemn prayers on Good Friday have been
revised accordingly.

'Finally, those who have not yet received the gospel

are related in various ways to the People of God'. Among
them the Constitution puts first the Jews, "the people to
whom the covenants and promises were given and from
whom Christ was born according to the flesh"; then the
Moslems; then "those who in shadows and images seek the
unknown God"; then all who strive to live a good life
according to their lights. Finally there are those who, deceived
by the Devil, "have become caught up in futile reasoning
and have exchanged the truth of God for a lie . . ." and those
"who, living and dying in a world without God are subject
to utter hopelessness. The Church painstakingly fosters her
missionary work to procure the salvation of all such men,
mindful of the command of the Lord "Preach the gospel to
every creature".'

Such is the picture of the whole Church, its relations with
others and its mission which the Vatican Council presents.
Among the People of God are chosen those who are to serve
them and fulfil this mission in the hierarchy; and there are
the laity with their special duties and opportunities.

## The Bishops' Charter

The third chapter of the Constitution deals with the hierarchical structure of the Church and is the most important
in so far as it affects the power of the Papacy. It begins by
reaffirming all the teaching of the First Vatican Council
'about the institution, the perpetuity, the force and reason
for the sacred primacy of the Roman Pontiff and of his
infallible teaching authority'. Then it goes on to the distinctive purpose of this Council 'to declare and proclaim
before all men its teaching concerning bishops, the successors
of the Apostles, who together with the successor of Peter,
the Vicar of Christ and the visible Head of the whole Church,
govern the house of the living God'.

It begins by saying that Christ formed his Apostles 'after
the manner of a college or a fixed group' (whence the
unbeautiful term 'collegiality' is derived), 'over which He
placed Peter chosen from among them'. The Apostles'

mission was confirmed on the day of Pentecost. Since it will last until the end of the world, they 'took care to appoint successors in this hierarchically structured society . . . They therefore appointed such men and authorised the arrangement that, when these men should have died, other approved men would take up their ministry'. This is the doctrine of the apostolic succession of bishops, who share by episcopal consecration the special outpuring of the Holy Spirit on the apostles. They are the high priesthood, and ordinary priests are simply described as their assistants.

We then come to the involved passages dealing with the relation of Pope and Bishops, somewhat reminiscent of the tongue-twisting definitions of the Trinity in the Athanasian Creed ('and yet there are not three gods but One God').

> 'Just as, by the Lord's will, St. Peter and the other apostles constituted one apostolic college, so in a similar way the Roman Pontiff as the successor of Peter and the bishops as successors of the apostles are joined together.
>
> 'The college or body of bishops has no authority unless it is simultaneously conceived in terms of its head . . . and without any lessening of his power of primacy over all, pastors as well as the general faithful. For in virtue of his office, that is as Vicar of Christ and pastor of the whole Church, the Roman Pontiff has full, supreme and universal power over the Church. And he can always exercise this power freely'.
>
> 'Together with its head, the Roman Pontiff, and never without this head, the episcopal order is the subject of supreme and full power over the universal Church . . . This college, in so far as it is composed of many, expresses the variety and universality of the People of God, but in so far as it is assembled under one head, it expresses the unity of the flock of Christ'.
>
> 'The supreme authority with which this college is empowered over the whole Church is exercised in a solemn way through an ecumenical council. A Council is never ecumenical, unless it is confirmed or at least accepted as such by the successor of Peter . . . The same collegiate power can be exercised in union with the Pope by the bishops living in all parts of the world, provided that

the head of the college calls them to collegiate action, or at least so approves or freely accepts the united action of dispersed bishops, that it is made a collegiate act . . . This collegiate union is apparent also in the mutual relations of the individual bishops with particular churches and with the universal church'.

'Although the individual bishops do not enjoy the prerogative of infallibility, they can nevertheless proclaim Christ's doctrine infallibly. This is so, even when they are dispersed around the world, provided that, while maintaining the bond of unity among themselves and with Peter's successor and while teaching authentically on a matter of faith or morals, they concur in a single viewpoint as the one which must be held conclusively. This authority is even more clearly verified when, gathered together in an ecumenical council, they are teachers of faith and morals for the universal Church . . .'

'This infallibility with which the divine Redeemer willed His Church to be endowed in defining a doctrine of faith and morals extends as far as extends the deposit of divine revelation . . . This is the infallibility which the Roman Pontiff, the head of the college of bishops, enjoys in virtue of his office, when as the supreme shepherd and teacher of all the faithful, who confirms his brethren in their faith, he proclaims by a definitive act some doctrine of faith or morals. Therefore his definitions of themselves, and not from the consent of the Church are justly styled irreformable . . . They need no approval of others nor do they allow an appeal to any other judgment'.

'Bishops govern the particular churches entrusted to them as the vicars and ambassadors of Christ . . . The pastoral office or the habitual and daily care of their sheep is entrusted to them completely. Nor are they to be regarded as Vicars of the Roman Pontiff, for they exercise an authority which is proper to them . . . Their power, therefore, is not destroyed by the supreme and universal power. On the contrary it is affirmed, strengthened and vindicated thereby'.

It has been necessary to quote these passages because, clear as they may be to theologians, it is not easy for ordinary people to understand how both one person and many persons can have supreme power. While the exceptional position of the Pope seems to be safeguarded in these definitions it is precisely the contention that he must act only in a corporate capacity (i.e. as head of the Bishops' College) that has caused his judgments in recent years on morals (e.g. the regulation of births and priestly chastity) and faith (e.g. the Eucharist and his 'Credo of the People of God') to be defied, or disregarded to an extent which would have been unthinkable before the Council. In fact the down-grading of the Papacy was, historically, the most serious consequence of the Council; and it is only too easy to see how in a few years it has contributed to the disintegration of that general confidence in authority which has for centuries been the distinguishing feature of Roman Catholicism.

The remaining chapters of the Constitution, on the Laity, on Religious, on the Eschatological nature of the Pilgrim Church and her union with the Heavenly Church – with its justification of the invocation of the Saints – and the very beautiful chapter on the rôle of Mary in the mystery of Christ and the Church, give rise to no novel ideas.

# Chapter 4

# Certain innovations and consequences

The Decree on Ecumenism certainly introduces a new attitude for, in addition to the duty of praying and working for the unity of all Christians, the Council admits that 'men of both sides were to blame' when speaking of the Reformation and the emergence of large communities separated from full communion with the Catholic Church. 'Yet the sin of separation cannot be imputed to those who are at present born into those Communities'. It is the object of the Ecumenical movement to overcome the many and serious obstacles to full ecclesiastical communion. 'Nevertheless all those justified by faith through baptism are incorporated in Christ. They have a right to be honoured by the title of Christian and are properly regarded as brothers by the sons of the Catholic Church'. In this spirit, the essential unity of Faith with the Orthodox Churches who also have the Apostolic Succession, and many merits of the separated Churches of the West, the Anglican Church in particular, are recorded and an impetus is given to sincere dialogue, with reunion as the ultimate goal. This is the main task of the Secretariat of Christian Unity, already established by John XXIII, whose activities we shall notice in Part Five.

In the decree on the *Pastoral Office of Bishops* we may notice particularly the recommendation of a pastoral council of clergy, religious and lay people in each diocese to assist the Bishop, which has proved in some cases to be a valuable form of cooperation, while in others it is more than the thin end of the wedge for the introduction of democracy and a good deal of interference with faith and order, as the Dutch experience shows. On the other hand the powers of the Bishop are greatly increased at the expense of parish priests, whose security of tenure disappears, as do all other limitations of the Bishop's freedom to remove or appoint clergy as required. It is desired also to end any system of patronage or nomination of bishops by civil authorities, which involves an attempt to revise certain Concordats, notably that with Spain.

## National Episcopal Conferences

Finally and most important, episcopal conferences are to be set up in each country, a development to which the Holy See was long averse.

> 'An episcopal conference is a kind of council in which the bishops of a given nation or territory jointly exercise their pastoral office by way of promoting that greater good which the Church offers mankind, especially through forms and programmes of the apostolate which are fittingly adapted to the circumstances of the age'.

Diocesan bishops and coadjutors are full members. Legates of the Roman Pontiff (Nuncios and Apostolic Delegates) are excluded. Each Conference may decide whether or not to allow auxiliary bishops deliberative or consultative status.

> 'Decisions of the episcopal conference, provided they have been made lawfully and by the choice of at least *two thirds* of the prelates who have a deliberative vote . . . and have been reviewed by the Apostolic See, are to have juridically binding force . . .'

It is also laid down that in special circumstances bishops of many nations may establish a single conference, as has been done in South America; but the prevailing tendency has been for the conferences to be national. They may legislate by a two-thirds majority subject to confirmation by Rome.

No doubt the vast number of the Catholic episcopate today explains this radical departure from the personal link of tradition between the individual bishop and the Holy See which the system of *ad limina* visits expressed. But this concession to nationalism, at a time when it is one of the most formidably divisive forces in the world, and the principle of decisions binding upon the faithful being made by majority vote are open to grave objections[9]. Among other things, it means that the ordinary priest or layman has no protection against the mediocrity and compromise which too often characterise majority agreements: his own bishop is reduced to a kind of member of parliament; the low standard of the vernacular liturgies imposed by various national hierarchies is an example of this. The obvious corollary is that the Synod of Bishops in Rome will inevitably consist mainly of delegates of the national conferences. The Catholic Church is in danger of becoming, organisationally, a kind of international federation or ecclesiastical United Nations.

## Modernisation in the Seminaries

In the Decree on *Priestly Formation* admirable dispositions are made for the reform of seminaries, in which students are to be prepared for the total dedication of the priesthood. In particular they should be very carefully trained for the state of priestly celibacy and 'warned of the very severe dangers with which their chastity will be confronted in present day society'. What is sad is that various steps to modernise discipline and the programme of studies, eminently reasonable on paper, should have been so quickly seized upon to allow the seminaries and theological faculties to be infected with all the disruptive and revolutionary ideas which are making chaos nowadays of the secular universities.

> 'The rules of discipline should be applied in accord with the age of the students so that they can gradually learn to govern themselves, to make wide use of their freedom to act on their own initiative and energetically, and can know how to work along with their confreres and lay people as well'.

*See note by Archbishop Lefebvre page 39.

'Students should also be conversant with contemporary philosophical investigations, especially those exercising special influence in their own country, and with recent scientific progress. In this way, thanks to a correct understanding of the character of modern times, students will be properly prepared for dialogue with the men of their own day'.

What in fact has happened, especially since seminarists have in many cases been allowed to exchange their clerical costume for jeans, or any old clothes and to mix on equal terms with their contemporaries, is that this famous dialogue has turned into a means of enrolling ecclesiastical students in one after another of the progressive causes and political enthusiasms of the moment. Class war, Maoism, the advocacy of violence to overthrow capitalist society, anti-war (i.e. anti-American) demonstrations, and the defiance of Papal teaching on all aspects of sexual morality – all these are rife, not only in the Netherlands and in France – the Franciscan novitiates being notorious – but in most other European countries and in the Americas. In view of all this there is a certain irony in the subsequent directive from Rome that Marxism should be studied in all seminaries. African seminaries seem to be immune from this turbulence.

It is difficult to find in the *Decree on the Renewal of the Religious Life* any cause of, or explanation for, the extraordinary laxity in observing the rule in many religious orders, the loosening of discipline and the way in which Jesuits, Dominicans, Franciscans, Augustinians and others have been plunging into public controversy, not to speak of the drying up of vocations and the abandonment of vows, which is, to the layman, probably the greatest scandal of the moment. Yet there are other orders, such as the Salesians, the Missionary Orders and some Benedictine families, who seem to retain their sanity, though they are all suffering from defections. The Decree calls for a renewal involving '(1) a continuous return to the sources of all Christian Life and the original inspiration behind a given community, and (2) an adjustment of the community to the changed conditions of the times', while observing the basic principles of chastity, poverty and obedience. 'Each should make its own and foster in every possible way the enterprises and objectives of the Church in such fields as these: the scriptural, liturgical, doctrinal, pastoral, ecumenical, missionary and social'. The manner of living, praying and working should be suitably re-examined and outmoded regulations suppressed. It is for the general chapters of the orders to issue norms and pass laws for appropriate renewal and 'to allow for a right amount of prudent experimentation'. Even the manner of living of the contemplative orders should be revised.

The general liberty to make changes has induced an impatience with old standards. No doubt the notable decline in the singing of the Divine Office, which liberty to recite it in the vernacular has brought about, the substitution in men's monasteries of a single vernacular Concelebration for the daily Masses hitherto celebrated by each priest, and the laicizing of dress, have all contributed to the general cheapening of monastic standards, which make the situation so painful to members of the community who are faithful to their traditions.

## Celibacy and Family Planning

In view of the outcry against priestly celibacy which has been filling the press and which, though most extreme in Holland, has been taken up in most of the White Men's countries, it is worth recording what the Vatican Council itself had to say on the subject in the *Decree on the Ministry and the Life of Priests*. After stating that 'the Church has always held in especially high regard perfect and perpetual continence on behalf of the kingdom of heaven. Such continence was recommended by Christ the Lord', the Council recognises that, while bishops and monks in the Eastern Churches observe celibacy, 'there also exist married priests of outstanding merit'. They go on, however to praise the celibacy of priests,

> 'consecrated to Christ in a new and distinguished way. They more easily hold fast to Him with undivided heart. They more freely devote themselves to Him and through him to the service of God and men . . . For these reasons, celibacy . . . in the Latin Church was imposed by law on all who were to be promoted to sacred orders. This legislation to the extent that it concerns those who are destined for the priesthood, this holy Synod again approves and confirms'. It also 'exhorts all priests, who trusting in God's grace, have freely undertaken sacred celibacy in imitation of Christ, to hold fast to it magnanimously and wholeheartedly'.

There can therefore be no question that, while Pope Paul VI reserved for himself a definitive exposition of this subject, he was fulfilling the purpose and spirit of the Council in drawing up his Encyclical *Sacerdotalis Caelibatus*, which he issued in June 1967. Cardinal Suenens now contends, however, that since a full debate on celibacy was not permitted in the Council itself, this decree (for which he no doubt voted) was not properly conciliar.[10]

The long Pastoral Constitution *Gaudium et Spes* contains, in its references to nuclear warfare, the Council's one outright condemnation,

> 'Any act of war aimed indiscriminately at the destruction of entire cities or of extensive areas along with their population is a crime against God and man himself. It merits unequivocal and unhesitating condemnation'.

Though the Constitution covers every aspect of human society from the family to the community of nations, re-affirming the Church's social teaching and in particular respect for the dignity of human personality, it has not, I think, given rise to any subsequent controversy, with one exception. That is the rather cautious paragraph on family planning.

---

[10]Interview with Monsieur Fesquet of *Le Monde*, 12 May 1970.

'This Council exhorts all to beware of solutions contradicting the moral law, solutions which have been promoted publicly and privately, and sometimes even imposed. For in view of the inalienable human right to marry and beget children, the question of how many children should be born belongs to the honest judgment of parents. The question can in no way be committed to the decision of government. Now since the judgment of the parents supposes a rightly formed conscience, it is highly important that every one be given upright and truly human responsibility. This responsibility respects the divine law and takes account of circumstance and the times'. Then after calling for better educational and social conditions and the provision of full moral training, it adds,

'Human beings should also be judiciously informed of scientific advances in the exploration of methods by which spouses can be helped in arranging the number of their children. The reliability of these methods should be adequately proven and their harmony with the moral order should be clear'.

It was perhaps not unnatural that, in view of this passage and the knowledge that Pope John XXIII had already brought into being a commission to examine the subject, some modification of the Church's ruling against contraception was anticipated. Hence the outburst when in 1968 Pope Paul eventually issued his Encyclical *Humanae vitae*, maintaining the prohibition of any artificial form of birth control.

## Anti-Semitism repudiated

It was in the discussion of the *Declaration on the Relation of the Church to non-Christian Religions* that the Council faced the general desire to condemn any form of anti-Semitism. For a time it seemed that *real politics* would prevent an outright statement of this kind, since Cardinal Tappouni, speaking for himself and four other Eastern Patriarchs, deeply conscious of the involvement of their Christian Arab peoples in the Arab-Israeli conflict, feared the consequences to their pastoral work of any pro-Jewish statement. Eventually this was overriden and a long passage was adopted basing on Scripture the unique 'bond linking the people of the New Covenant with Abraham's stock'. After recalling that Christ, the Virgin Mary and the Apostles were all Jews, it goes on to say:

> 'since the spiritual patrimony common to Christians and Jews is thus so great, this sacred Synod wishes to foster and recommend that mutual understanding and respect which is the fruit above all of biblical and theological studies and of brotherly dialogue'.

Then comes the declaration that what happened in Our Lord's passion cannot be blamed upon all the Jews then living, without distinction, nor upon the Jews today, and repudiation of what had undoubtedly been the anti-Jewish attitude of the mediaeval Church, such as the restrictive canons of the 4th Lateran Council of 1215 A.D. dealing with the Jews.

> 'The Church repudiates all persecutions of any man. Moreover, mindful of her common patrimony with the Jews, and motivated by the gospel's spiritual love and no political considerations, she deplores the hatred, persecutions and displays of anti-Semitism directed against the Jews at any time and from any source'.

After the expected denunciations of this Declaration in the Arab press, controversy on this closing of an unhappy chapter died away.

### Conscience

Finally the *Declaration on Religious Freedom*, to which great importance was attached especially by American Catholics, is certainly a new departure in the Church's teaching. The main purpose is to establish the right of freedom for religious belief, expression, organisation, teaching and practice as against the interference of governments – of which atheistic Communist governments are now the most notorious. But the whole case is rested in this article on natural law and is applied, not exclusively to the Catholic Church or to Christians, but to all organised religions.

'Injury therefore is done to the human person and to the very order established by God for human life, if the free exercise of religion is denied in society when the just requirements of public order do not so require'.

The case is argued on the basis of the essential rights of man and of the family, parents 'having the right to determine, in accordance with their own religious beliefs, the kind of religious education that their children are to receive'.

But there is a passage which progressives and radical theologians have since seized upon to justify the freedom of Catholics to follow their conscience against the magisterium of the Church itself:

'God calls men to serve Him in spirit and in truth. Hence they are bound in conscience, but they stand under no compulsion. God has regard for the dignity of the human person whom he himself created: man is to be guided by his own judgment and he is to enjoy freedom'.

There is indeed no novelty in teaching the right and obligation of a man to obey his conscience – and also the duty to see that his conscience is rightly informed. But it is evident that, taken at its face value, anyone in a defiant spirit can use this statement to pull to pieces all that the Council had to say about obedience to ecclesiastical authority. Which is exactly what many opinionated Catholics are so busy doing today to the detriment of the unity and credibility of their Church.

# APPENDIX

## THE SNARES OF 'COLLEGIALISM'

*Extract from a statement by Archbishop Marcel Lefebvre, former Superior General of the Holy Ghost Fathers*[11]

'Garaudy said, speaking to the university students of Louvain a few years ago: "We shall only really be able to collaborate when the Church has modified her teaching, and her kind of authority"; he could hardly have put it better. And, knowing as we do that

---

[11] 'Published in *Forts dans la Foi* No. 4 (Revue trimestrielle de Catéchèse Catholique), May-June 1968.

for the Communists and technocrats seeking to dominate the world, the one obstacle to mankind's subjection is the Catholic Church of Rome, we shall not be surprised at the joint efforts made by Marxists and masons to modify the Church's magisterium and hierarchical structure.

The winning of a victory in the Near or Far East is an appreciable thing. But the paralysing of the Church's magisterium and the modifying of her constitution would represent an unprecedented victory. It is not enough to conquer a people to do away with their religion. Religion is often thereby driven deeper. But ruin the faith by corrupting the magisterium, stifle personal authority by making it dependent on a maze of organisms easy to infiltrate and influence, then the end of the Catholic religion may indeed appear possible. For this 'assembly-magisterium' can be manipulated so as to insinuate doubts into every problem of the faith, and such a decentralised teaching authority will paralyse the Roman centre.

It is easy to see that such astute attacks sustained by the world press, even the Catholic, make it possible to conduct widespread propaganda campaigns disturbing and unsettling people's minds and turning God's commandments, the Creed, the sacraments, the entire catechism upside-down. We already have blatant examples of this.

Once the magisterium is decentralised it loses its direct control over the content of faith; the multiple theological commissions of the various episcopal assemblies are slow in coming to decisions, since their members are divided in opinions and over methods.

Ten years ago, and even more so 20 years ago, the personal magisterium of the Pope and the Bishops would at once have reacted, even if, among the Bishops and theologians, some were not in agreement. Nowadays the magisterium is at the mercy of majorities; it is paralysed, prevented from intervening promptly, and such interventions as it is allowed to make are watered down to the point of ineffectiveness, so as not to offend any member of the commission or assembly concerned.

This democratisation of the Church's magisterium is a deadly peril, if not for the Church, which has always God's protection, then for the millions of helpless faithful whose minds are being poisoned without any antidote being forthcoming from the doctors.

It is sufficient to read the reports of these assemblies at every level to realise that what may be called the "collegiality of the magisterium" amounts to its paralyzation. Our Lord called *persons* to feed His sheep, not collectivities. The Apostles and their successors obeyed the Master's command, and so it has continued until the present century. It was not until the present period that we heard talk of a Church *in permanent Council, in a continual state of collegiality*. Results have not been slow in coming: all is now topsy-turvy – faith, morals, discipline. There is no need to look for examples, which could be multiplied *ad infinitum* if space permitted.

Paralysis or weakening of the magisterium: the latter is apparent from the lack of definition of ideas and terms employed. There is such a remarkable lack of precise and necessary distinctions that one no longer knows what words mean. Terms such as human dignity, liberty, social justice, peace, conscience may from now on, within the Church herself, be allowed a Marxist or a Christian sense with equal conviction.

Democratisation of the magisterium is naturally followed by democratisation of Church government. Modern ideas being what they are, it has been still easier here to obtain the desired result, carrying these ideas over into the Church by means of the slogan of "collegiality". The Church's government had to be "collegialised": the Pope's power must be shared with an episcopal college, the government of each bishop with a priests' college, and the parish priest should share the running of his parish with a pastoral college of the laity; all hedged about by commissions, councils and assemblies . . . who must all have their say before the various authorities may think of issuing orders or directives . . .

But if the Pope has personally retained a certain freedom of government, how can one fail to affirm that the episcopal conferences limit it singularly? Several instances could be cited of the Holy Father's having gone back on a decision during recent years under pressure from an episcopal conference. Now the Pope's authority applies not only to the Bishops but also to the faithful, and the Pope alone has power of jurisdiction over the whole world.

A far more obvious consequence of collegial government is the paralysing of the individual bishop's authority in his own diocese. Many are the reflections on this subject coming from bishops themselves, and they are highly instructive. Theoretically, a bishop can, in a number of cases, act against the vote of an assembly, at times even against a majority unless the vote is submitted to the Holy See. But this proves to be impossible in practice. As soon as the episcopal assembly ends it session, its decisions are published, and are then known to all priests and faithful. What bishop can, in fact, oppose these decisions without thereby showing himself at odds with the episcopal assembly, and at once finding himself up against hot-headed persons, who will invoke the authority of the assembly against him? The bishop has become the prisoner of this collegiality, which should have remained a limited organ of consultation and joint deliberation, instead of becoming a decision-making body[12] . . .

This present collegialism is being applied also within the diocese, within the parish, within religious Congregations and in every community of the Church in such a way as to make the exercise of government impossible: authority itself is constantly frustrated.

As soon as one introduces elections, parties spring up, and consequently division. When habitual government is subjected to consultative voting in its normal exercise it is rendered ineffective. The collectivity itself is then the first to suffer, as the common good can no longer be pursued efficiently and energetically'.

---

[12]To give an example, in a diocese where I was not long ago visiting our communities, the Bishop most hospitably came to meet me at the station, apologised for not being able to put me up at his residence, took me to the minor seminary. There I found stairs and corridors swarming with young men and women. On enquiring if the young men were seminarians, the Bishop answered, with a deep sigh: 'Alas, no. You must please understand I do not agree with their being in my seminary, but the episcopal conference decided we must hold young men and women's Catholic Action meetings in our minor seminaries. These young trainee catechists have been here for the past week. What can I do? I can hardly act differently from the others'.

# PART THREE

# Changes in Worship

# Chapter 5
# The Council's Constitution
# on the Liturgy

It is necessary in order to understand the new form of worship which has been introduced in the Western Catholic Church and the reactions which it has provoked, to compare, in the course of this section, the Mass authorised by Paul VI in 1969 with that which had existed with minimal changes for at least thirteen centuries and was given its definitive form by St. Pius V in 1570 after the Council of Trent. This will, I fear, be uninteresting to non-Catholic readers but cannot be avoided.

The difficulty is that, while the Tridentine Missal is complete and self-contained – with the Order of Mass, the chants, prayers and readings for every Sunday and major feast and season, the Proper of the Time and of the Saints throughout the year, the votive masses and the calendar, together with prayers of preparation and thanksgiving and exact rubrics – we have as yet no such compendium to compare with it. What we have available so far is the Apostolic Constitution of April 1969, the new Ordo with its alternatives, General Instruction, the new Calendarium Romanum and a Lectionary containing scripture readings for a three year period. The Proper of Saints is yet to come, with Masses for special occasions. The available books are extremely expensive and the full Latin texts are hard to come by both for priests and people; at present few parishes or religious communities possess them, with the result that a visiting priest of another nationality is unable to say Mass unless he happens to be fluent in the local national language.

Even at solemn celebrations one can see the celebrant dodging about between two or three books. There is so far no complete Catholic 'Book of Common Prayer'.

We have yet to see the revised Breviary containing the daily Office, built around the psalter, which regular and secular clergy are supposed to recite. This may well take another two or three years to produce, and the new formulas for the sacraments of Baptism, Confirmation, Penance, Marriage, Ordination and Holy Unction are in the process of completion. There is much criticism of this confused and untidy launching of the liturgical changes, most of all, of course, among the many Catholics who saw no real need for them.

A further difficulty of comparison arises from the fact that, whereas the Latin of the Tridentine Missal was the universal language of worship, with more or less exact translations familiar to the laity, it is nowadays only the vernacular version of the new services which is experienced by the vast majority of the faithful. It is dissatisfaction with the idiom, style and tendentious character of the Anglo-American text devised by the International Committee on English in the Liturgy Inc., which is greater among priests and people in this country, for instance, than criticism of the relatively unknown new Latin text.

The *schema* of the Constitution on the Sacred Liturgy was debated from 22 October to 13 November 1962 by the Vatican Council and passed next day. There was very little definite opposition but a good many amendments were considered and accepted; the final Constitution was promulgated a year later. With almost indecent haste and long before any new service books could be produced, the new Consilium on the Liturgy, under the radical Cardinal Lercaro, started issuing directives for change. These were almost all negative and abolitionist, such as suppression of the genuflexion which had always marked particular veneration of the record of the Incarnation of Jesus Christ in the Nicene Creed, and of the opening words of St. John's Gospel, which were read at the end of each Mass, when priest and congregation had also been accustomed to kneel at the words *Et verbum caro factum est*. In addition most of the genuflections and signs of the cross performed by the celebrant were cut out; and a whole lot of advices were given in favour of abolishing the existing ornaments of the Altars, scrapping the Communion rails to encourage the practice of standing to receive Holy Communion, celebrating at altar tables facing the people and the moving of tabernacles.

The psychological effects of these arbitrary instructions were disastrous. They presented the liturgical reformation to devout Catholics as something essentially negative and destructive and designed to diminish rather than emphasize the importance both of the Incarnation and of the real presence of Christ in the Eucharist. Simultaneously they gave the green light to those, on the other hand, who were straining at the leash to free public worship from the stuffiness of mystery, history and tradition and make it more congenial to modern man, who is not disposed to 'bend the knee'. A number of radical 'experiments' were made by avant-garde priests with episcopal connivance. We have noticed above some of the deplorable results in the Church of the resulting feuds. It is a pity; because, when the definite Order of the revised Mass began to appear about six years later, it was evident that a number of positive improvements had been introduced, whatever else might be criticised.

But the harm had been done. It was the consequence of allowing lobby methods to prevail. An organised lobby, political or religious, which develops enthusiasm for a doctrine and slogans of its own, is always in a hurry. But in a matter of legislating for the worship of hundreds of millions of people, accustomed to a rite of millenial antiquity, which had given rise to so many habits of prayer, thought, action and art forms through the centuries, there was no need to hurry. Nor, surely, was there any justification for a series of arbitrary shocks. Had it not been for the Council, the gradual introduction of improvements in the sacred rites, such as those begun by Pope Pius XII in his revision of the Holy Week services, and a judicious extension of the use of the vernacular, could have been done with the necessary detachment and deliberation by the Holy See. The fact that the liturgical lobby captured the Council at an early stage meant that its spirit and methods soon became dominant throughout the mechanism of the universal Church, the more so as the present Pope, Paul VI, is evidently inclined personally both to extreme austerity in worship and to its 'socialisation', which are two of the features most characteristic of the movement.

The liturgical movement, as it is called, has been growing in momentum in the last 50 years. For a long while it mainly took the form of explaining the venerable origins and meaning of the Eucharistic liturgy, without any particular desire to change it, and particularly to encourage the intelligent participation of the faithful in it. From the time of Pope Pius X's insistence at the beginning of the 20th century on children becoming communicants at an early age, the merits of frequent communion were insisted upon, culminating in the reforms of Pius XII who, by reducing the period of fasting – which used to be from midnight – to one hour only before receiving the Sacrament and so allowing Mass to be celebrated at any hour of the day, produced an immense increase among those for whom attendance at Mass normally meant communicating themselves. Those were the days when – to mention one or two examples – Dom Cabrol, the Abbot of Farnborough, and the Abbey of St. André near Bruges produced complete missals for the people in Latin and in their own languages, which ran into editions of hundreds of thousands, with comments and instruction upon the liturgy itself and notes for every season and saint's day. The Benedictine Abbey of Collegeville in Minnesota more recently fulfilled the same function in the United States. Special Holy Week books also became popular. Great scholars, such as Father J. A. Jungmann, s.j., produced careful and accurate studies of the fascinating origins of the

Roman rite from post-apostolic times, the various modifications which had occurred since the Canon itself had taken its definite form at the end of the 6th century under St. Gregory the Great, the relations and differences between the Western and Eastern liturgies, the codifying work of the Council of Trent, and so on. Several more popular works of equally high standard, such as the Abbé François Amiot's *History of the Mass*, had put the fruits of this scholarship within the reach of the intelligent Catholic reader.

What, however, characterised the liturgical movement, as we knew it at that time, was its *pietas*. A limited number of minor improvements designed to clarify the ceremonies were suggested – such as rearrangement of the *fraction* or breaking of the consecrated Host and the prayers for peace after the Lord's Prayer, put forward by Dom Capelle in 1941 and adopted in the recent reforms. But there was no disparagement of the historic formation of the Eucharistic service in the days of the Roman persecutions and nothing but respect for the early martyrs – and only martyrs, with the exception of the Mother of God – whose names were venerated in the Canon.

What gave a modernising and radical turn to the liturgical movement was the eager propaganda of the vernacular Mass societies, which were quite small groups originally in European countries but became a considerable influence in the United States, with all the technique and temptations of publicity proper to that country. Insistence on the proposition that the average worshipper should understand every word of what was said in the celebration inevitably involved disregard of antiquity in itself and national prejudice against distinctively Roman features. One heard for the first time the names of early martyrs, such as St. Lucy and the other six brave young women who suffered atrocious tortures and execution for the faith and whose names occur in the Canon, described as 'that list of Roman worthies'. It was a school of thought which increasingly stressed congregational simplicity and participation as the main criterion and was as *impious* (in the Latin sense) as the older scholars were *pious*. These two elements, as well as some personalities already engaged in the simplification of the calendar and the reforms of the Paschal observances at the Vatican, were represented in a Liturgical Conference held at Assisi in 1956. Its members were mostly drawn from Germany, France, Belgium, Holland and the United States. There was thus a corps of enthusiasts ready to fill the pre-Conciliar Commission on the Liturgy formed under the Chairmanship of Cardinal Cicognani. It did not take them very long to work out the *schema* or draft of the Constitution which was ready when the Council met. Many of the same group worked together through the Council and found their way into the Liturgical Consilium set up to implement the principles which it adopted. The innovating, modernistic elements – particularly American officials of the I.C.E.L., such as Father Sigler, its Secretary General, who repudiated the doctrine of Transubstantiation – in this body were increased in the process and they have enjoyed much of the boosting of 'progressives' by the apparatus of publicity which we shall see at work in Chapter 8, though a certain number of Bishops representing Episcopal Conferences, appointed or coopted to join the Consilium, attempted to apply the brake. Eventually, as one of the latter has said 'After four years of discussion something had to be decided'. It is fairly evident that the nucleus of the reforming party had in fact decided at an early stage what they wanted and were determined to push it through; the 'Mini-mass' which they demonstrated in the Sistine Chapel during the first Synod of Bishops was little different, despite the raising of episcopal eyebrows, from the *Missa Normativa* eventually promulagted in 1969. And the dominant figure of the whole proceeding, who had been Secretary of the Liturgical Commission of Pius XII, then of the pre-Conciliar Committee, then of the Consilium which fabricated the reforms and then of the Congregation of Divine Worship, is Mgr. A. Bugnini. His influence with the present Pope is very great. He is evidently a man *tenax propositi* and has had the advantage at a critical time of a particularly ineffective and docile chairman. He is as much the architect of the new Mass as was Cranmer of the Communion Service in the Book of Common Prayer, with which comparison is inevitable, since their radical alternatives to the same Roman missal have much in common.

## The Constitution on the Liturgy: the Changes envisaged

The following are the principal passages of the Constitution on the Sacred Liturgy which explain the changes which have now been made in the Mass and the objectives which they are designed to serve.

'The liturgy is the summit toward which the activity of the Church is directed; at the same time it is the fountain from which all her power flows. For the goal of apostolic works is that all who are made sons of God by faith and baptism should come together to praise God in the midst of his Church, to take part in her sacrifice and to eat the Lord's supper'.

'It is the duty of pastors of souls to ensure that the faithful take part knowingly, actively and fruitfully'.

'In this restoration (of the liturgy) both texts and rites should be drawn up so that they express more clearly the holy things which they signify. Christian people, as far as possible, should be able to understand them with ease and to take part in them fully, actively and as befits a community'.

However 'There must be no innovations unless the good of the Church genuinely and certainly require them; and care must be taken that any new forms adopted should in some way grow organically from forms already existing'.[13]

'The rites should be distinguished by a noble simplicity; they should be short, clear and unencumbered by useless repetitions; they should be within the people's powers of comprehension and normally should not require much explanation'.

'In sacred celebrations there is to be more reading from holy Scripture and it is to be more varied and suitable'.

---

[13] A provision which in several respects has, as we shall see, been flagrantly disregarded.

## Use of Latin and the Vernacular

'Particular law remaining in force, the use of the Latin language is to be preserved in the Latin rites' (as distinct from the rites of the Uniate Eastern Churches). But since the use of the mother tongue, whether in the Mass, the administration of the sacraments or other parts of the liturgy, may frequently be of great advantage to the people, the limits of its employment may be extended. This extension will apply in the first place to the readings and directives, and to some of the prayers and chants . . . It is for the competent territorial ecclesiastical authority mentioned in Articles 22 and 23 ('territorial bodies of bishops legitimately established') to decide whether, and to what extent, the vernacular language is to be used . . .; their decrees are to be approved, that is confirmed by the Apostolic See . . . Translations from the Latin text into the mother tongue which are intended for use in the liturgy must be approved by the competent territorial ecclesiastical authority'.

This permission to use the vernacular in Masses celebrated with the people is repeated later but the following qualification is added,

'Nevertheless steps should be taken so that the faithful may also be able to say or sing together in Latin those parts of the Ordinary of the Mass which pertain to them'.

This refers mainly to the responses, Confiteor, Kyrie, Gloria, Credo, Sanctus and Agnus Dei.

## Other innovations

Another paragraph provides for the restoration on Sundays and Holy Days of the 'prayer of the faithful', now called the Bidding Prayer in English. 'By this prayer in which the people take part, intercession will be made for the whole Church, for the civil authorities, for those oppressed by various needs, for all mankind and for the salvation of the entire world'.

Another section extends fairly widely permission for concelebration, hitherto confined to Ordinations. A new rite has been devised for this purpose. Several priests, or even an entire community of religious, can thus join with a principal celebrant in consecrating the Bread and Wine, stretching out their right hand toward them and reciting together the words of consecration. This has, of course, reduced very greatly the number of Masses offered in monasteries. It is seldom performed in parishes and missions, where each priest has, more often than not, two or even three Masses to say for the people on a Sunday.

We need not here examine the directions given for revising the rites of other sacraments, except to note that instead of the 'conditional baptism' hitherto administered to converts, implying doubts about the validity of baptism in non-Catholic Churches, there is the recognition of baptism wherever administered as admission to the Christian 'People of God'.

> 'A new rite is also be to drawn up for converts who have already been validly baptised; it should indicate that they are now admitted to Communion with the Church'.

## Shortening and vulgarisation of the Divine Office

The Council introduced a number of relaxations regarding the Divine Office, that is to say the Hours (Matins, Lauds, Prime, Terce, Sext, None, Vespers and Compline) which choir monks and nuns have hitherto been obliged to sing or recite together each day, while secular priests read them in their Breviary. In the first place, the number of hours is to be reduced. One may spare a passing tear for the abolition of Prime, the morning office which gave its name to the Prymer, the first popular prayer book in English, which appeared first in the 15th century. It contains the beautiful prayer, so familiar to all Church of England people, which Cranmer incorporated in the Book of Common Prayer: *Domine Deus Omnipotens qui ad principium hujus diei nos pervenire fecisti.* 'O Lord, our heavenly Father, Almighty and Ever-lasting God, who has safely brought us to the beginning of this day, defend us in the same with thy mighty power . . .' etc. Prime was also the morning office commonly recited by Benedictine oblates. Of the three following hours, Terce,

Sext and None, the Council allows priests other than choir monks in future to say one only.

> 'The hour known as Matins, although it should retain the character of nocturnal praise when celebrated in choir, should be adapted so that it may be recited at any hour of the day; it is to be made up of fewer psalms and longer readings'.

Secondly, the length of the hours is to be reduced,

> 'So that it may really be possible in practice to observe the course of the hours proposed in Article 89, the psalms are no longer to be distributed throughout one week but through some longer period of time'.

This will probably be a month, the system adopted by Cranmer in his Morning and Evening Prayer, in line with the proposals of the Spanish Cardinal Quizones in his revised breviary of 1535.

Thirdly,

> 'In particular cases and for a just reason, ordinaries (bishops) can dispense their subjects wholly or in part from the obligation of reciting the divine Office, or may commute the obligation . . . The Latin language is to be retained by clerics in reciting the divine Office. But in individual cases the ordinary has the power of granting the use of a vernacular translation to those clerics for whom the use of Latin constitutes a grave obstacle to their praying the Office properly'. He also 'has the power to grant the use of the vernacular in the celebration of the divine Office even in choir, to nuns and members of institutes dedicated to acquiring perfection . . . Any cleric bound to the divine Office fulfils his obligation if he prays the Office in the vernacular tongue together with a group of the faithful'.

The nett result of all these dispositions is, first, to lessen the amount if time spent in prayer and worship and secondly, by destroying the tradition of the sung Latin both in the Mass and the Choir offices, to reduce the solemnity and mystery of the services and in particular of the Gregorian Chant in religious houses. No doubt there is much to be said on practical grounds for shortening the breviary, so fas as busy parish clergy are concerned; but it is the *shift of emphasis* away from the primary obligation of prayer for religious, that seems to many to be a cheapening of a particular richness of the Catholic tradition.

One would think, from reading the Council texts, that the vernacular was to be the exception rather than the rule in the language both of the Mass and of the Office. On the contrary, no sooner was the door ajar than it was pushed wide open by the episcopate in most countries under the impulse of progressives. Within four years it was impossible in Lisbon – to take a typical Catholic capital – to find a single Mass said in Latin, except, by special concession, in the Chapel of the Knights of Malta, the vernacular being imposed by authority. It is the same in most of Western Europe and the Americas, though here and there, where choirs refuse to be silenced, it is still possible to find a Solemn High Mass or Missa Cantata decently performed in Latin. The Bishops of England and Wales have been more sympathetic than most hierarchies, except the Polish, to the retention of Latin for a certain number of Masses. In Poland the Latin Mass prevails in most parishes, the vernacular being associated by the people with the communist-sponsored 'peace priests'.

As for the Office, the permissions and dispensations mentioned in the Council's Constitution have been liberally sought and granted and that not only to clerics who are no Latinists, but to whole communities, so that one finds even Benedictine abbeys, the very home of liturgical tradition, who ought to know better, enacting an English, French or German caricature of the venerable services, to the ruin, of course, of the chant for which they were famous. Again there are many practical and human arguments for being 'with it' in this way. And human nature is such that, once a rule, hitherto sacrosanct, is breached, it is easy to justify more and more liberties. There are only too many convents now, notably in the Netherlands and France, in which the recitation of the Office has quite fallen into dissuetude and where irregular attendance at a concelebrated vernacular Mass once a week or fortnight is all that remains of what was hitherto a most sacred daily obligation. There are certainly religious houses which have adapted themselves with a good heart to the liturgical innovations and have retained the spirit of their rule. There are certainly Benedictine abbeys in which renewal has been combined with the best of the old order and in which the sense of a dedicated and happy community has been preserved.

No doubt it is not mainly the loosening and desacralisation of the routine of community worship which accounts for so many friars leaving their orders and so few recruits joining the novitiates. It is the impact upon these intellectual communities of the literature of theological speculation and scepticism and the libertarian propaganda of the IDOC variety[14], which have a more dissolvent effect, together with the varieties of Marxism which their younger members tend to absorb from their contacts in the world. Yet a firm and exacting rule of community worship was a wonderful anchor for the monk; and *lex orandi* is *lex credendi*.

## The Liturgical Year

The pre-eminence of Sundays over all celebrations, except for major feasts of Our Lord, is the keynote of the proposals for the reform of the Church's year.

> 'The Lord's day is the original feast day, and it should be proposed to the piety of the faithful and taught to them in such a way that it may become in fact a day of joy and of freedom from work. Other celebrations, unless they be truly of overriding importance must not have precedence over this day, which is the foundation and nucleus of the whole liturgical year'.

The process of reducing the number of saints' days, and in particular of the festivals which could replace Sundays, had started before the Council and now the Catholic Church has swung from one extreme – the excess of feast days – to the other which, for the ordinary Sunday churchgoer, means their virtual exclusion. To take a striking example; until a

---

few years ago, during the summer holidays one often came upon a Sunday Mass celebrated with red vestments because it was the feast of an apostle, such as St. James, or St. Matthew or St. Bartholomew, instead of the invariable green. Nowadays, except for the tiny minority attending weekday Masses, no practising Catholic ever assists at the Mass of any Apostle throughout the year, with the solitary exception of S.S. Peter and Paul, where their feast is a holyday of obligation. Further, as we shall see, whereas in the old Mass the names of all the Apostles were given and venerated in the most sacred part, the Canon, while S.S. Peter, Paul and Andrew were invoked in other parts, the names of all of them (as well as those of all other saints except the Blessed Virgin, who rates a single mention) are deleted from the new texts of the revised liturgy. Thus, while the Council gave an immense amount of attention to the importance of the Apostles, upon whose authority the much-emphasized powers of the bishops were based, it is probable that before long most Catholics will not even know who they are.

# Chapter 6

# The New Mass Examined

Let us now see how the Liturgical Consilium, which has been at work since the adoption of the Constitution, has carried out the provisions that 'the rites should be distinguished by a noble simplicity; they should be short, clear and unencumbered by useless repetitions' and the other provision for more scripture readings. Obviously these and the requirement of popular intelligibility were susceptible of maximum or minimum interpretations. While the inspiration of the Holy Ghost is claimed for the Council as a whole, literal inspiration could hardly be asserted and it is not credible that He should be responsible for the proposal that the Eucharistic service should be even shorter than the existing Low Mass, which was already a very short service. It is more likely that this provision combined the firm intentions of two bodies of reformers – the liturgical purists who were inclined to suppress every prayer and action which was not found in the most primitive post-Apostolic texts, and the modernists who were for scrapping all that was not congenial to contemporary sentiment. The result was a mighty debate for four years, in which moderate conservative voices had a mildly restraining effect, and in which the ecumenical desire to attenuate any features of the Eucharist which might give offence to Protestants came to play a considerable part. There was a struggle, for instance, to retain *any* offertory prayers, instead of simply placing the bread and wine on the altar without any word; and only at the last moment was the beautiful dialogue between priest and people, in which he asks them to pray that his sacrifice and theirs may be acceptable to God the Father, saved from the scrap heap by an urgent appeal to the Pope. The outcome, in the form of the Mass said with the people on Sundays – for this weekly Church parade is all that is now insisted upon – is, it must be admitted, a rather dull little service. Allowing for three lessons, instead of the previous two, the homily, bidding prayer and the administration of Holy Communion to, say, a hundred people, it is all over in 40 to 45 minutes. Except for the pause during the Communion and a few minutes silence afterwards – a provision often skimped if the priest has more than one Sunday Mass to say – there is not a moment for private concentration and prayer. That, despite all the 'high falutin' talk of the renewal initiated by the Vatican Council, is about all that the Catholic religion really amounts to now for the majority of practising Catholics. When, however, the new rite is sung in Latin at a solemn celebration, as it is in a few churches, since the old Roman *graduale* (the chanted Introit, Gradual, Offertory and Communion antiphons) can be used and certain ceremonies are retained, as well as the Gregorian, or polyphonic settings for the familiar parts, its divergence from the old Mass is not so noticeable.

While many sincere criticisms of the deletions from the liturgy have been made by devout Catholics (who, it must be remembered, have never had a word to say in this liturgical reform, which from first to last has been a clerical imposition), defenders of the Tridentine Mass are wrong in asserting that there is anything positively heretical in the text of the new rite. Though lacking aesthetic or literary merit, it has certain admirable features that are above criticism. The provision of three lessons[15], one normally from the Old Testament, one from the New (Epistles, Acts or Apocalypse) and the third from the Gospels, is a return to the Old Roman Mass of early centuries. In the new Lectionary the readings are spread over three years, so making the

---

[15] On Sundays and principal feasts.

faithful familiar with much of the Bible as a whole, as was not the case with the fixed yearly epistles and gospels. Another excellent innovation is the act of contrition, as it is called, or rather an invitation to pause and recall one's sins before the general confession, though in fact this only takes half a minute. Another is the interval of silence, which we have mentioned, after the Communion, when it is observed. Minor improvements are the suppression of the practice by which the celebrant continued to read parts of the Mass to himself while they were being sung, and the placing of the dismissal *Ite Missa Est* after the blessing. A most important reform is the re-introduction of Communion in both kinds for communities and on a number of special occasions, subject to episcopal regulation, without alteration of the doctrine that Christ is wholly present under either species.

It is, however, what has been *taken out*, from the preparatory part of the Mass and its conclusion, from the offertory and from the central part of the Eucharistic liturgy itself – in the form of the new alternative Eucharistic prayers which, by an extraordinary innovation, may be used and are indeed recommended for use, in replacement of the Roman Canon – that causes justifiable fears. I give examples in the next chapter, for those who are interested, of the texts which have been suppressed or mutilated. I will deal here with four features of the excisions which appear to have some doctrinal significance.

## 1. Disappearance of the Holy of Holies

The 'Prayers at the foot of the altar' have been suppressed. These were a solemn preparation for entering into the holy place recited by the priest and his ministers at the entrance to the sanctuary and, more recently, in dialogue with the congregation. While the Western Church has not observed the symbolism of entering into the Holy Place of the Temple in Jerusalem as have the Eastern Churches, in which the priests go beyond the Iconastasis to celebrate the Eucharistic mysteries unseen by the people, the notion of this solemn entry to the place of sacrifice was preserved in these opening prayers. '*Introibo ad altare Dei*' said the priest after invoking the Trinity. This was followed by the Psalm *Judica me*, from which that verse was taken and repeated at the end. Then the priest said the *Confiteor*, confessing his sins to God, the Saints and the people around him, asking them to pray for him, who in turn repeated it, asking for his prayers. The absolution '*Indulgentiam, absolutionem et remissionem peccatorum vestrorum*' with the sign of the Cross, followed, and was commonly regarded as absolving from venial sins in preparation for Communion. Then, after some versicles and responses, the celebrant said his first *Oremus* and went up to the altar saying the prayer *Aufer a nobis*. 'Take away from us we beseech thee, Oh Lord, all our iniquities that we may be worthy to enter with pure minds into the Holy of Holies through Christ our Lord'. He then kissed the altar saying 'we beg Thee, Oh Lord, by the merits of thy Saints whose relics are here and of all the Saints, mercifully to forgive all my sins'.

This ceremony of humble access, which dates from an early Frankish practice and was inserted in the missal of the Roman Curia by Innocent III in about 1200 A.D., had come to be looked upon as an essential introduction to the Mass and all the people knelt for it. Now all this is destroyed. '*Introibo ad altare Dei*' said one of the martyrs of the French Revolution, the Abbé Noel Pinot as, dressed in his eucharistic vestments with his hands tied behind his back, he mounted the steps to the guillotine at Angers. Something more than symbolism is lost in the abolition of these prayers at the foot of the altar, nor does a short greeting uttered by the priest facing the people from his chair, followed by an abbreviated confession recited together standing, compensate for the loss. But, of course, if the altar is simply a bare table in the middle of a bare hall, with no sanctuary or altar rails, there is nowhere visible to enter.

## II. The Sacrifices of the Old Testament and the New

A more serious omission is that of all mention of the sacrifices of the Old Testament in the new Eucharistic prayers. In the Roman Canon immediately after the consecration, the celebrant offers 'the pure, holy and immaculate Victim, the bread of eternal life and the chalice of everlasting salvation' to God the Father, saying,

> 'Vouchsafe to look with favourable and serene countenance upon them as thou didst deign to accept the gifts of thy just servant Abel, the sacrifice of our Patriarch Abraham and what thy high priest Melchisedech offered to Thee, a holy sacrifice, a spotless victim'.

This passage recalls the great doctrine of the priesthood of Christ developed by St. Paul in Chapters V to X of his Epistle to the Hebrews, in which he identifies our Lord as him of whom God said 'Thou art a priest forever according to the order of Melchisedech', and shows that he replaced the sacrifices of the old law by the sacrifice of His own blood. 'Having therefore, Brethren, in the entering into the holies by the blood of Christ, a new and living way which He hath dedicated for us through the veil that is His flesh, and a high priest over the house of God, let us draw near with a true heart, in fullness of faith . . .' It is difficult to understand the motivation of those who suppressed this passage with all its implications, unless it be that the modern American (for instance) is thought to be incapable of understanding what is meant by the word sacrifice in its real historic sense, of which the supreme example was Christ's sacrifice of his life on the Cross. One has the feeling that when the word is retained, as it is once or twice, in the revised rite, it can be taken to mean simply an offering or tribute like Cranmer's 'this our sacrifice of praise and thanksgiving'.

## III. Banishing the Saints

A third series of deletions, which can have no meaning except as a concession to Protestant sentiment, is the removal of every saint's name (except that of the Blessed Virgin) throughout the revised service. Confession of sins was made at the start of the Mass not only to God and to those present but also to our Lady, the Archangel Michael, St. John the Baptist, Saints Peter and Paul and all the Saints. That has disappeared, though in the shortened Confiteor Blessed Mary and 'all the Angels and Saints' are asked 'to pray for me'. However this is only optional as the priest can leave out the Confiteor all together if he likes. Again at the end of the Offertory the oblation was offered to the Holy Trinity in memory of the passion, resurrection and ascension of our Lord Jesus Christ and in honour of Blessed Mary, ever Virgin, of blessed John the Baptist, the holy apostles Peter and Paul and all the saints' *ut illis proficiat ad honorem, nobis autem ad salutem; et illi pro nobis intercedere dignentur in caelis, quorum memoriam agimus in terris'*. This whole prayer, redolent of belief in the union between the Church triumphant and the Church militant which runs all through the old missal, has been abolished.

Then we come to the Canon, the central Eucharistic prayer with the unprecedented choice of four texts which, except for the actual narrative of the Institution at the Last Supper, which is common to all, differ considerably. In the old Roman Canon which may still be used, if desired – that is the one serious concession to tradition – a considerable list of saints is venerated and their merits and prayers invoked just before the consecration. Most of their names are nowadays printed, however, in brackets and may be omitted. They include St. Mary, St. Joseph (thanks to Pope John XXIII), the eleven original Apostles, four of the early successors of St. Peter – all of them martyred, St. Laurence, the deacon, and five other early Roman martyrs, of whom few details are known. All this probably dates from before the conversion of the Empire when the persecution of Christians was vividly remembered. Another list occurs towards the end of the Canon after the Memento of the Dead, in the prayer 'to us sinners also, hoping in the multitude of thy mercies, grant some part and society with thy saints'. Here are mentioned S.S. John the Baptist, Stephen, the first martyr, the coopted Apostles Matthias and Barnabas, four other men and seven women who gave their lives for the Faith. This is just one of these untidy relics of early pious additions to the primitive Eucharist which the modern reformer delights in wiping away. Thus in the new Eucharistic Prayers, II, III and IV all these martyrs are erased. All that remains of the Saints in No. II (which takes about 3 minutes to say) is 'make us worthy to share eternal life with Mary the Virgin Mother of God, with the apostles and with all the Saints who have done your will throughout the ages' – a modest Anglican formula. In III there is a similar request to share in the inheritance of the Saints and the principle of invoking them is saved by the addition of the words 'on whose constant intercession we rely for help'. There is no mention of this in IV.

## IV. Mass Intentions

The sacrifice of the Mass is always offered on behalf of the whole Church, but it has become an immemorial practice to offer it also in order to apply the merits of the Passion of Christ to individual people living or dead or for other particular causes. These are called Mass Intentions, for in the Roman Canon the priest is instructed to recall in silence for a few moments the names of those for whom he intends to pray (*pro quibus orare intendit*) both in the Memento of the Living which precedes the Consecration and in the Memento of the Faithful Departed which follows it. And at the end of the Mass, in a prayer now abolished, he begged the Holy Trinity to grant 'that the sacrifice which, unworthy as I am, I have offered in the eyes of thy Majesty may be acceptable to Thee and propitious (*propitiabile*) to me and to all on whose behalf I have offered it'. The faithful have always given the priests fees or offerings for Masses offered for their special intentions. This is a most intimate and human link between personal and family needs and the Eucharistic sacrifice. No doubt it has often been the cause of certain abuses; but who are we to complain, as we admire and still worship in churches, chantries and chapels built in the age of faith in which Masses were to be celebrated for the souls of donors, their relations or forbears? Nowadays, if one's mother has died, or one's child is sick, or one's wife about to undergo an operation, or if any particular anxiety is to be faced or special need supplied, the first instinct of the practising Catholic in many countries is to ask a priest to offer a Mass for that intention.

Now this practice was the main aversion of the 16th century Reformers who, teaching 'justification by faith' alone, could not admit that salvation was to be gained through grace received in visible sacraments. It was the great aim of Cranmer to destroy belief in the efficacy of the Mass for salvation. For as he wrote in 1550[16],

> 'The very body of the tree, or rather the roots of the weeds, is the popish doctrine of transubstantiation, of the real presence of Christ's flesh and blood in the sacrament of the altar (as they call it) and of the sacrifice and oblation of Christ made by the priest for the salvation of the quick and the dead'.

What is now disturbing is to find all mention of persons living and dead excluded from the newly devised Canons (II, III and IV)[17]: there is no pause for this purpose. Nor is any reference to the offering of the Holy Sacrifice for the living and the dead to be found anywhere in the new Ordo. Taking this fact, together with the exclusion of the veneration of the Saints to which I refer above, it is impossible not to conclude that the deliberate purpose of the Liturgical Consilium has been to conciliate the traditional Protestant prejudices on these two points[18]. The desire to assist the movement for the possible reunion of the churches by omitting any external practices, not having doctrinal importance, which might unnecessarily upset non-Catholics is an ecu-

---

[16] In *The Defence of the True Catholic Doctrine of the Sacrament.*
[17] Except that the name of a dead person may be recalled in a Mass for the dead.
[18] A representative of the Westminster Diocesan Liturgical commission giving a demonstration of the new Mass, when it was introduced, in the Cathedral, asked the congregation to note that there was 'nothing in it to which our separated brethren can object'.

menical motive deserving of sympathy. It is a very different matter when, as in this case, it involves for Catholics as a whole an important matter of Faith.

So what we have now is something unknown in the history of the Catholic Church, namely alternative methods of celebrating the most sacred part of the Eucharist with different doctrinal implications, a truly Anglican comprehensiveness. In the old Roman Canon, retained in the teeth of opposition from the Protestant element in the Liturgical Consilium owing to the Pope's insistence, we have not only the full familiar veneration and invocation of the Saints, but also the pauses, which I have indicated, in which the special intentions of Mass for the living and the dead are observed. In the alternative Canons, which Pope Paul himself unhappily suggested as the price of preserving the old one, both these features are omitted. What is the effect upon priests and faithful? In some areas, the diocese of Plymouth in England, for instance, we find young monks, evidently echoing advices from the Liturgical Office in Rome, going around the parishes declaring that Mass intentions are abolished. Yet in parishes of my acquaintance, in the dioceses of Portsmouth and Birmingham, in the same country, Mass intentions, for which parishioners have doubtless made offerings, are regularly announced in advance for every day of the week as usual. It is arguable that, unless priests pray the old Roman Canon, instead of the shorter Eucharistic prayers, which many bishops recommend them to use especially on weekdays, they are receiving money for Mass intentions under false pretences.

This is an extreme example of the confusion caused by the new liturgical reforms, or rather compromises. In the new Mass – no doubt since unanimity could not be reached in the Liturgical Consilium – there are three alternative forms of greeting at the start, three alternative 'acts of penance', four alternative 'acclamations' after the Consecration, and, more important, these four alternative forms of the Canon or Eucharistic Prayer itself. This surely is no way to strengthen unity.

# Chapter 7
# Rubrics and texts

We have hitherto examined the new Order of Mass in the light of its history and the apparent objectives of its authors, and we have noticed in earlier pages the varied reactions to it of the Catholic people as a whole. We cannot leave the subject without considering its effect upon the many priests whose whole life hitherto has been built around the exact and carefully ordered celebration of the Mass.

Let us look first at the general character of the celebration as it is now presented in the General Instruction, issued on Easter Sunday 1969, which replaces the General Rubrics and the *Ritus Servandus in celebratione* of the Tridentine Missal[19]. It states,

> 'The Lord's Supper is the assembly or gathering together of the people of God, with a priest presiding, to celebrate the memorial of the Lord . . . The Table of the Lord is the table of God's word and Christ's body and from it the faithful are instructed and refreshed'.

– a strange statement this, since the whole of the 'Liturgy of Word' as it is now called, including the scripture readings, has been completely removed, in the new order, from the altar table to the president's chair or a lectern.

This, no doubt, is an adequate description of the service for most Protestant Christians – though certainly not for Anglo-Catholics. But, to the Catholic priest as we know him the Mass is something more than a memorial meal preceded by Bible readings; and we have to read through several

---

[19]But see Postscript, page 74.

pages, in which the priest is referred to as the president of the assembly (a title for which antique precedent is found in St. Justin Martyr's description of the Eucharist in the 2nd century), before we arrive at any recognizable reference to the Eucharistic Sacrifice. 'Christ instituted the memorial of his death and resurrection at the Last Supper. This is continually made present in the Church when the priest, representing Christ, carries out what the Lord did. When he instituted the paschal sacrifice and meal he handed it over to his disciples for them to do it in his memory'.

The emphasis throughout, however, is on the preparation, consumption and clearing up of a meal. The bread to be used, according to the Latin rite, is still be to unleavened and made of wheaten flour, though great liberties have already been taken with this in Holland and elsewhere where fragments of the consecrated bread are handed round in baskets. 'The nature of the sign demands that the material for the eucharistic celebration appear as actual food. The Eucharistic bread, even though unleavened, should therefore be made in such a way that the priest can break it and distribute the parts to at least some of the faithful. When the number of communicants is large or other pastoral needs require, small hosts may be used'.

The kind of bread used is purely a matter of ecclesiastical discipline and this shows an admirable desire to return as far as possible to the conditions of the Last Supper. But here and in the statement that 'it is most important that the faithful should receive the body of the Lord in hosts consecrated at the same Mass', there seems to be an unrealistic disregard of the sensible developments of many centuries and the practical requirements of today. The use of compressed wafer breads is a neater and tidier practice than the distribution of crumbling fragments to the vast numbers of communicants of modern times (10,000 Communions a week, for instance, in the single Cathedral parish of Westminster), and in most parishes it is impossible for the priest to gauge in advance the exact number of those who wish to communicate. Hence the recourse to hosts consecrated at a previous Mass and reserved in the eucharistic tabernacle to supplement those newly consecrated, a convenient practice universal until a year or two ago, and still general in this country, which does not cause the least misunderstanding to priest or people, since it is the same Lord who is received in either case.

This raises the important point of doctrine recalled by the Pope in his Credo, but entirely ignored in this Instruction, that this same 'unique and indivisible existence of Christ the Lord . . . remains present after the Sacrifice in the most Blessed Sacrament which is reserved in the tabernacle, the living heart of our churches'. What, then, is to be done with any fragments or particles of the consecrated elements that remain? According to the Calvinist view, adopted by Cranmer, who ruled that the curate should have any remaining bread or wine 'for his own use', the Lord's presence exists only in the heart of the receiver; and much of the Dutch Church is now impregnated with Calvinism. The new Dutch catechism, veering in that direction, considers it absurd to suggest that the Real Presence remains in small crumbs or dust of bread. But the Catholic tradition is clear; '*Tantum esse sub fragmento quantum toto tegitur*', as St. Thomas put it in the *Lauda Sion*. Consequently in the old Mass the most reverent care was taken to place any remaining particles in the tabernacle, unless, there being no tabernacle, the priest consumed them, and to collect and consume in the ablutions any crumbs remaining on the corporal, in a ciborium or on the people's paten. Further, any remains of the sacred Blood were similarly consumed by the priest in the ablution of the chalice with wine and water, poured over his fingertips, before drying it with the purificator. While doing so he said the beautiful prayers '*Quod ore sumpsimus*' and '*Corpus tuum Domine quod sumpsi et sanguis quem potavi*' which have been suppressed in the new Ordo. All that we read in the new Instruction is 'After communion the priest (or deacon if there is one) returns to the altar and collects the remaining particles'. It does not say what he is to do with them. 'The vessels are cleansed by the priest or deacon after the Communion or after the Mass. The chalice is washed with wine and water, or with water only, which is then drunk by the priest or deacon'.

This is typical of the extreme looseness of the new rubrics compared with the most exact rules of the Tridentine Mass which, in view of the sacred character and function of the celebrant, governed his every gesture of head and hands, adapting them to symbolic expressions of prayer, praise, concentration, or adoration. Very little of this remains. There is little regret for the suppression of the excessive number of genuflections and signs of the Cross; but such acts of worship as the splendid raising of the priest's arms as, standing at the head of his people before the altar, he intoned the *Gloria in excelsis*, or the raising and joining of his hands as he invoked the blessing of Almighty God the Sanctifier on the oblations, or the raising of his eyes to God at the beginning of the Canon, are examples of the centuries-old practices which the new Puritanism has abolished. At his ordination, the priest's hands had been anointed with holy oil and bound together with linen preparatory to his authorisation to offer the Holy Sacrifice. Whenever he stood with hands joined together, as at the beginning of Mass, he was enjoined to do it thus *'junctis manibus ante pectus, extensis et junctis pariter digitis, et pollice dextero super sinistrum posito in modum crucis'*; and from the Consecration until the ablutions he had to keep the thumb and forefingers of each hand joined together, except when actually handling the Sacrament. I give these exact and, to the modern, finicky examples, to show the discipline of ordered symbolism which in the old Mass subordinated the personality of the priest to his divine function. There is a language of hands; nothing is more irritating to the audience at a theatre than to watch actors who do not know what to do with their hands. And the Mass is a sacred drama.

No doubt most priests trained in the old rite instinctively use the same meaningful gestures in the new. One trembles to think of the behaviour of their successors, even if they do not wear long hippie hair as may be seen in photographs of recent Ordination groups in the United States. Nor is it only a matter of gestures; there are a number of lacunae in the new Ordo which are, I believe, just as instinctively filled by the older priests with their accustomed formulae. For example it is stated that the use of incense is optional at the beginning of the Mass, at the Gospel and at the Offertory but no words are provided for its blessing or use. '*Ab illo benedicaris in cujus honore cremaberis*' was the blessing for the first two occasions, and one of the most beautiful prayers of the Mass was provided for the third – the incensing of the oblations and the altar, '*Per intercessionem beati Michaelis*',

> 'Through the intercession of blessed Michael the archangel, who stands at the right hand of the altar of incense, and of all his elect, may the Lord deign to bless this incense and to accept its sweet fragrance: through Christ our Lord. Amen'.

Then as the priest censed the bread and wine, he continued:
> 'May this incense, which has been blessed by thee, rise up to thee, oh Lord, and may thy mercy descend upon us'.

While he censed the altar he said verses 2-4 of the 140th Psalm.

> 'Welcome as incense smoke let my prayer rise up in thy sight, Lord: may the lifting up of my hands be accepted as the evening sacrifice. Lord, set a guard on my mouth, a barrier to fence in my lips, lest my heart turn to words of evil to cover sin with excuses'.

Then returning the thurible to the deacon or minister he said,

> 'May the Lord kindle within us the fire of his love and the flame of everlasting charity'.

Is it because our separated brethren dislike invoking St. Michael and the saints (they do not like incense anyway) that this lovely passage is scrapped or is it simply the dislike of poetic imagery? These blessings, as well as the two prayers said at the ablutions, could perfectly well be restored to accompany and give significance to the celebrant's actions without affecting the shortness of the new Mass or the people's participation in most of it, which seem to be the chief preoccupations of the official reformers.

The same desire to de-mystify and shorten may, I suppose, account for the mangling of the following beautiful old prayers. The first was that said by the deacon or priest before reading the Gospel *Munda cor meum*,

> 'Cleanse my heart and my lips, Almighty God, who didst cleanse the lips of the prophet Isaiah with a live coal. In thy gracious mercy deign so to cleanse me that I may be able fitly to proclaim thy Holy Gospel, through Christ Our Lord, Amen'.

This becomes in the new dispensation simply,

> 'Almighty God cleanse my heart and my lips that I may worthily proclaim your Gospel'.

The second, which is of great antiquity, was said as the priest put wine and a drop of water into the chalice at the offertory. Here it is in its Elegant Latin,

> 'Deus, qui humanae substantiae dignitatem mirabiliter condidisti et mirabilius reformasti, da nobis per hujus aquae et vini mysterium ejus divinitatis esse consortes qui humanitatis nostrae fieri dignatus est particeps, Jesus Christus, Filius tuus, Dominus noster, Qui tecum vivit et regnat in unitate Spiritus Sancti, Deus per omnia saecula saeculorum'.

This is now condensed into,

> 'By the mystery of this water and wine may we come to share in the Divinity of Christ who humbled himself to share in our humanity'.

Apart from the cutting out or shortening of so many parts of the Mass which, as well as having a symbolic significance, had become part of the aesthetic and literary heritage of Christian civilisation, priest and faithful alike in English-speaking countries have to endure the clumsiness of 'translations' provided by the International Committee on English in the Liturgy, authorised by the Holy See. Among the fads of this synthetic Anglo-American language is the assumption that people are too moronic to understand the relative participle; so everything has to be broken up into jerky sentences. Thus '*Agnus Dei qui tollis peccata mundi, miserere nobis*' becomes 'Lamb of God. You take away the sins of the world. Have mercy on us'; and the Committee's version of the Roman Canon, instead of being a continuous prayer to God the Father, is similarly fragmented. To take the most sacred part, '*ut nobis Corpus et Sanguis fiat dilectissimi Filii, tui Domini nostri Jesu Christi, qui pridie cum pateretur, accepit panem . . .*' is rendered '. . . let it become for us the Body and Blood of Jesus Christ, your only Son, our Lord (stop). The day before he suffered he took bread . . . etc.'.

Here are a few instances of the graver liberties taken by the I.C.E.L. In the Confiteor the famous words '*mea culpa, mea culpa, mea maxima culpa*', retained in the Latin of the new Mass, are simply cut out in the English. '*Orate fratres ut meum et vestrum sacrificium acceptabile fiat . . .*' is rendered, so as to obscure the special sacrificial function of the priest, 'Pray brethren that *our* sacrifice may be acceptable'. As for quotations from the Gospels, they are altered *ad lib*. Thus '*pax hominibus bonae voluntatis*' in the Gloria (Luke I v. 21) becomes 'peace to men who are God's friends'. At the consecration of the chalice Christ is made to say, not 'my Blood which shall be shed for many'[20] (Matthew XXVI v. 28, Mark XIV v. 24), but 'my Blood which shall be shed for all men'. At the communion, instead of the words of the centurion (Matthew VIII v. 8) '*Domine non sum dignus ut intres sub tectum meum . . .*', we have 'Lord I am not worthy to receive you'. And so on. The translations of the new Canons, which, despite the omissions we have noted, are indeed beautiful

---

[20]The Greek words in the Gospels are perfectly clear  To render those words as 'for all' would, according to St. Thomas Aquinas (Summa III G 60, Art 6), be 'a forgery of our Lord's words'; and the Council of Trent taught 'though He died for all, yet all do not receive the benefit of His death, but only those to whom the merit of His passion is communicated', and the reason why the words 'for all' were not used are explained in the Catechism which it authorised. The present repudiation of this doctrine is now explained by the Congregation for Divine Worship on the grounds that according to exegetes the Aramaic word used at the Last Supper (though there is, of course, no record in this language, the Greek codices being the earliest available) had the sense of 'for all' or for the multitude. It seems that, the courting of the modern world being now the order of the day, Our Lord's words also said at the Last Supper 'I pray not for the world, but for them which there hast given me, because they are Thine' (John XVII 9) are no longer very popular.

and eloquent inventions, and a good English version of the Bible is used for the lessons.

Everything mentioned in this chapter is of course a *detail* compared with the basic elements of the Eucharistic sacrifice and Communion which the revised rite retains, and for this reason, as well as because of obedience to the Pope who has imposed it, the vast majority of priests will carry it out loyally and make the best of it, even in its bowdlerised English, or other vulgar tongues. Obviously this must also be the spirit in which practising Catholics as a whole participate in this common act of worship. To some its plainness, freedom from traditional ceremonies, imagery and mystery and its popular and social character undoubtedly appeal; and there will be a slowly growing number of young priests who know no other Mass. But something intangible and precious will have been lost to the Christian world; and we know of very many priests who are acutely distressed at the destructive character of many of the changes, and who are convinced that the full and intelligent participation of the faithful and the other advantages of the new order could be attained without the impious jettisoning of the valued and significant acts and words, which I have indicated. It is not unreasonable to hope that they may be restored. It is not a good thing for the Church to take the heart out of her most devoted priests.

## POSTSCRIPT

The observations made in this and the preceding chapter refer to the Order of Mass and its General Instruction issued 'with the force of law' by the Pope in April 1969. This is in general use at the time of writing. The Latin text of the new Missale Romanum, produced by the Vatican Press in the following year, contains, however, a few changes, particulars of the new Calendar, the new Propers for Sundays and saints' days and – what is more important – a revision of doctrinal passages in the General Introduction. It will probably take a year or more for this to filter down to most parishes, depending upon the time required for approved vernacular translations to be printed, and the cost. For the purchase of constantly changing service books has become a real burden for the unfortunate parish priest.

It seems that there has been a perceptible reaction against the Protestant tendencies which were discerned in the earlier version. I am indebted to *The Association for Latin Liturgy* for the following comments,

> 'The General Introduction is prefaced by an entirely new *proemium*. This is noteworthy in that it relates the revised liturgy to the teachings both of the Council of Trent and Vatican II, and thereby answers much criticism that the new rite implied certain doctrinal shifts. In it we find reaffirmed (Para 3) the doctrine of the Real Presence of the Lord (*proesentia realis Domini*) effected through transubstantiation (*per transubstantionem*) by the words of consecration . . .
>
> One modification is the restoration of the priest's prayer *Quod ore sumpsimus* after the Communion . . .'

Father Crehan S.J. makes the following observations.

> 'What is entirely to be praised about the new missal is the corrective it administers in the *Institutio Generalis* to the unbalanced language of the *Ordo Missae* issued a year ago. In that document one was told, "The Last Supper, at which Christ instituted a memorial of his death and resurrection, is made to be continually present in the Church, when the priest . . . does what Christ himself did". Now at the same place (para 48) one reads, "At the Last Supper Christ instituted a sacrifice and paschal banquet by which the Sacrifice of the Cross is made continually present in the Church when the priest . . . does what Christ did". The change is one of substance in the right direction'.

Though the new book is called *Missale Romanum*, it is not, alas, the complete and compact service book which the old Missal was. It is a poor look-outfor the intelligent layman. Apart from the arbitrary swopping around of the familiar Sunday collects and other prayers, 80 Prefaces (instead of 15) and the bewildering variety of Sunday, commemorative or votive masses which a priest can use *ad lib* on a weekday, none of the epistles, or other Bible readings, or gospels is included. For these one must be armed with the large new lectionary containing readings with their intervening psalms for three years. An English 'People's Missal' including the Sunday readings for 3 yearly cycles has since been published. At a sung mass one would also have to grope for the old *Graduale Romanum* to find the gradual and Alleluia which precede the gospel of the day and the offertory chant. The price of allowing liturgical and archaeological pundits, as well as innovators, to have their head in producing the new books (under cover of the supposed advantages of 'pluralism') is this labyrinth, which can hardly be described as the 'short and clear rites . . . within the people's power of comprehension' which the Vatican Council envisaged. As Father Crehan concludes, 'The difficulties surrounding the production of a satisfactory Latin or bilingual missal for the use of the laity can now be fairly assessed'.

# PART FOUR

# The Anti-papal Movement

# Chapter 8
# The 'Conciliar Church' campaign

One of the main reasons for the disorder of the Catholic Church today, in the fields of morals, faith, authority and worship alike, is not only the power of the mass-media, but the distinctive features which they have developed in the process of moulding and professing to articulate public opinion in recent years. It is these features which have in turn helped to give form to the neo-modernist, anti-papal movement, which developed during the 2nd Vatican Council, and influenced its subsequent tactics.

The most relevant of these features to our subject is the assumption that all schools of thought and all actions concerning the conduct of human societies, whether temporal or spiritual, must be presented in the news as *progressive* or *reactionary*, the assumption being that the former are good, the latter bad. Historically one can trace this falsifying simplicity in the now dominant establishment of the press, television, radio and popular literature, to the alliance of Western liberalism with Communism precipitated by the Spanish Civil War in 1935-8. This alliance, cemented by the unnatural union of the Western Democracies and Soviet Russia during the Second World War, was only partially shaken by the Cold War which developed thereafter between East and West. The Communists had sold their categories and their vocabulary of the social revolution to the publicists, journalists and radio commentators of the West; and though the Americans, and for a time the British and Western Europeans, applied these criteria in defence of what they called 'the Free World', it was not long before the collapse of the Empires under the joint impact of Soviet and American anti-colonialism re-established the old partnership. The American religion of democracy was easily adapted to endorse every revolt against establis d authority or the old order, whether in the politics of Africa and Asia or in those of the Western World. 'Progress' and 'Liberation' became almost interchangeable terms.

It was inevitable therefore, when an Ecumenical Council of unprecedented size and an agenda so wide as to include every aspect of human behaviour and belief, became for four years a standard item of news, that the mass media should immediately apply their categories of progress and reaction to every sign of divided opinion among the Council Fathers. It was equally inevitable that those within the Council who kicked against the pricks of Papal authority should not resist the temptations of favourable publicity so lavishly offered to them. Thus in all the subsequent controversies concerning 'collegiality', the rights of national episcopates as against the Papal Curia, the defiance of tradition by daring theologians, the challenging of papal encyclicals on sexual morality or priestly celibacy, or the process of monkeying with the Mass, it is invariably the innovators and the rebels who get a good press. They are the 'progressives'.

This brings us to the second main feature of the modern mass media affecting our subject, which is the Sexual Obsession. 'Over-paid, over-sexed and over here' used to be the common description of American soldiery in the Old World. No doubt it was the American film industry and its attendant glossy magazines which originally popularised in Europe the preoccupation with sexual intercourse which had become the singular characteristic of a traditionally Puritan and enlightened United States; but it was not long before the collapse of family standards and traditional morality in England and the other Post-Protestant countries outdid the immodesty of the New World. To copulate with impunity soon came to be assumed, by those whose profession is to toady to the multitude, to be one of the fundamental rights of man – and the teenager. Contraception and abortion have become 'progressive'. Sex has become a primary interest for which every form of mass medium – the film, television, the press and the book trade – considers it necessary to cater. In this atmosphere – again unprecedented in history – it was to any prospect of the weakening of Christian doctrine about marriage and chastity that excessive attention was hopefully devoted both during the Vatican Council and during the subsequent tribulations of Pope Paul VI. While this sexual obsession is peculiar to North America and Western Europe, the Communist world and other continents are relatively free from it, except for the permeating influences of Western films and radio.

The third characteristic of the development of the modern mass media and especially television, which applies to the treatment of all news, is their increasing sensationalism. Not only violence, but also all that is shocking or suggestive of conflict or rebellion is picked out for description or visual display. This can, and often intentionally does, give a distorted picture of ecclesiastical as well as social and political events. It is one of the main means of deceiving the reader or the viewer into believing that vociferous minorities – be they militant students, African 'liberation movements', concupiscent clerics or priests who abandon their vocation – are really in the majority, when they are not.

This analysis helps to explain both why and how this vast apparatus of tendentious publicity impinged upon the Ecumenical Council itself in a way which John XXIII could not have foreseen, soon destroying the confidential character of the discussions which, as in former General Councils, the Fathers had promised to observe, and how it has since been used to promote the most powerful international agitation against Papal authority itself which has ever been organised within the Catholic community.

This agitation has two closely related centres. There

is the group of avant-garde intellectuals in the United States, who before the Ecumenical Council ended proclaimed themselves the new 'Catholic Establishment 'as against the then conservative episcopate of the country; and there is IDO-C, the 'International Centre of Documentation on the Conciliar Church', mainly Dutch in origin, whose ramifications extend to more than 30 countries. We shall examine each of these in turn.

## The New Catholic Establishment in the United States

The way to seize power, as Lenin well knew, is not to broadcast one's aspirations to all and sundry in the hope that a majority will spontaneously adopt them. It is to form a disciplined body of professional revolutionaries under the tight control of a small directorate, which decides when and how to use its resources to confuse and undermine the existing social structure, to create and then exploit the required revolutionary situation. It is this method which has been used, *mutatis mutandis*, by 'The Catholic Establishment' for the 'progressive terrorism of Catholic public opinion' – to use a Dutch expression – in the United States. This body, without openly denying the *magisterium* of the Papacy and the Episcopate, deliberately sets itself up as a rival authority. It is a relatively small, exclusive organisation of progressivist *illuminati*, most of them in control of, or in a position to determine the policy of, publications and other means of influencing opinion. It has come to exercise immense power not only through Catholic channels but – as we shall see in Europe also – by obtaining the support of key people in the secular mass-media.

Describing its power in one of its own reviews[21] John Leo writes, 'The birth control discussion in the United States for instance, was entirely an Establishment production'. As this was well under way in the early '60s, when the frustration of avant-garde *periti*, such as Hans Kung and the late

[21] *The Critic*, December 1966-January 1967.

Father Courtney Murray, to obtain satisfaction for their contraceptive enthusiasms in the Vatican Council itself already provided welcome fodder for a sex-ridden press, it was not surprising to find the Establishment orchestra in full blast against Pope Paul VI's Encyclical *Humanae Vitae* when it at last appeared in 1968.

According to Leo, quoting a former writer, Father John Hugo, the Establishment 'is a small coterie admiring one another's writings, although at times politely and tentatively disagreeing . . . who have seized all the microphones in a determination to speak for the Church'. He goes on to explain,

> 'The microphone-seizers are a loose but exclusive fraternity of several dozen scholars, journalists, activists and publishers. They write for and edit the most influential Catholic journals . . . They publish one another's manuscripts, warmly review one another's books, cite one another in lectures they invite one another to give, then collect the lectures and articles into books for yet another round of favourable discussion. The Establishment is liberal, progressive, largely urban, suspicious of institutions, anti-war[22] (but mostly non-pacifist), half clerical and half lay . . .
>
> The chief business of the Establishment is the shaping and publicising of the issues which will dominate American Catholic life. This is done largely through the six Establishment journals, all of them edited by laymen – the *National Catholic Reporter, Cross Currents, Jubilee, Commonweal, Continuum* and *The Critic*. They provide the links to the publishing houses, the campuses, the secular journals and the Protestant world, as well as to the lower-level publicists and periodicals which take their cue from the Establishment and function as transmission belts for Establishment ideas'.

What are those 'issues' and 'ideas'? *The Institute for Freedom in the Church*, which the Establishment has recently created, by its very title suggests them – the democratisation of authority, from parish to papacy; the loosening of the Church's moral imperatives so as to conform to the sexual

---

[22]Meaning, presumably, the war in Vietnam.

liberties prevalent in American society, and the substitution of heartiness and freedom of expression for awe and dignity in worship. Denunciation of the Papal Curia, opposition to any American bishop or religious superior who presumes to question the moral or theological vagaries of any of his subjects – the rebellious Berrigan brothers for instance, these and the boosting of news from Europe concerning any and every defiance of Papal authority and ecclesiastical discipline are matters on which it is easy enough to evoke support from 'The American way of life', which is encouraged to find itself at home in the freedom of the new 'Conciliar Church' as against the 'pre-Conciliar ghetto'. The unfortunate bishops are classed either as 'war-mongering prelates and reactionaries' – that goes for most of them – or 'peace-loving men of God' if, as a few do, they make themselves agreeable to the new Establishment.

Mr. Leo is good enough to give us an exact list of Establishment personalities. It will suffice here to make a selection: Michael Novak, author of *The Open Church*, William Birmingham, Editor of the *Mentor-Omega* paperbacks, Justus George Lawlor, Editor of *Continuum* and chief Editor of the important publishers Herder and Herder, Philip Scharper, the head of Sheed and Ward in America, and Wilfrid Sheed who, like several of the others mentioned, writes and works for *Commonweal*. 'Specialists' on birth control, marriage and contraception, such as John Noonan, figure prominently in the list of academic collaborators; and, of course, Archbishop Roberts, S.J., is listed as 'the Favourite'. The Establishment now controls the Catholic Press Association and two lecture agencies, University Speakers and National Lecture Service. It is well placed to use the opportunities which television offers and can depend upon the support of Father Lynch of Radio Vatican and Gerard Lemioux of Radio Canada. Its links with the secular press are well established by direct representation, as by John Cogley in the *New York Times* (he was its religious news editor during the Vatican Council) or David Meade in the *Chicago*

*Sunday Times*, and by assured editorial support in other national dailies and weeklies. The Catholic Establishment has many links, discussions and exchanges with Protestant leaders and with Zionist groups which help to increase its acceptability to a wider public, though it must be admitted that the ecumenical operation for which it is mainly known, the Centre for the Study of Democratic Institutions, which several of its leaders have helped to form under the Presidency of Robert M. Hutchins, has a singularly political and secularist flavour.

It is not difficult to understand how much this highly organised junta of Catholic radicals has contributed to alienating the younger priests from their Bishops in the United States. It may well be that the majority of the faithful, whose crowded parish churches used to be such a welcome tonic to their visiting coreligionists from the Old World, have retained their solid goodness. But, if so, they have, alas, no comparable 'public address system' to announce it.

## IDO-C

I have dealt in some detail with the mechanism and methods of the neo-modernist and anti-papal campaign in the United States, not only because of the size and wealth of the Catholic body in the most powerful country in the world, but because the United States is the main centre of the religion of democracy, which informs the post-Conciliar reformers throughout the world. The particular developments of the philosophical, theological and political trends of the last two decades in France which have undermined belief in objective realities and caused violent dissensions in the Church is another story[23]. A peculiar combination of spiritual pride, nationalism, Calvinism and the sexual obsession has produced the Dutch revolt against the Holy See which is the most serious, since the Netherlands so far is the only country in which the Catholic hierarchy has

---

[23]See Chapter 10.

formally identified itself with the revolt. The attempts to exploit the Conciliar 'renewal' in such a way as to diminish the teaching authority of the Pope and overthrow tradition in theology, ethics and worship, as well as reactions against these attempts, have indeed taken distinctive forms in many countries, notably of Western Europe, Northern and Latin America. What is important to realise is the existence of an international organisation which coordinates all the various national groups of progressive activists and reformers; assures simultaneous publication of news favourable to their enthusiasms or prejudices throughout the world; pours out a regular flow of doctrinal material independent of the official magisterium of the Church and, by operating from a centre in Rome, gives an apparently Catholic flavour to the whole enterprise. This is IDO-C, the International Centre of *In*formation and *Doc*umentation concerning the *C*onciliar Church. It describes its functions and organisation as follows[24],

> 'IDO-C seeks to continue the new "horizontal" com-
> munication sparked off by the Council between bishops
> and theologians, between different peoples and conti-
> nents, between Catholics and other Christians, between
> the Institutional Church and public opinion, thus putting
> in contact the opinions and thoughts of all members of
> the People of God. To guarantee this communication
> IDO-C has set up a committee composed of 120 theolo-
> gians, members of research institutions and religious
> correspondents in something like 30 countries'.

It goes on to record its indebtedness to 'two of the most important centres set up during Vatican II – the CCCC and the DOC'. It was in fact formed by a fusion of the two. DO-C was established alongside the Council as a centre of information for Dutch bishops (no doubt to keep them up to the mark) in December 1963. Its bulletins, first published in Dutch only, soon began to appear also in French, English, German, Spanish and Italian. CCCC, *C*entro di *c*oordina-zione delle *c*ommunicazione sul *C*oncilie, was formed about

---

[24]'Translation of its French information bulletin.'

the same time as a press bureau for 'progressive journalists' covering the Council. These people have the main responsibility, through their professional contacts with the press and the radio in many countries, for that arbitrary designation, to which I have referred, of the Council Fathers as 'reactionaries' and 'progressives', and was the main means of providing publicity for inspired leaks from any of the latter who lent themselves to such tactics and from the avant-garde *periti* or experts in the Council. When the Council ended, the journalists of CCCC joined forces with the Dutch centre, and IDO-C came into being in December 1965, under the presidency of a Belgian Dominican, Father Rafael van Kets, a professor at the Angelicum in Rome, and with a Dutch priest, Father Leo Alting von Geusau, as Secretary General. It is his busy peregrinations around the globe that seem to have been mainly instrumental in forming national sections of IDO-C or cells for the distribution of its literature. He now has an American executive director, furnished by the United States 'Establishment' to assist him.

Since 1968 IDO-C has not been so open in using its own title for these branches, except in the United States, partly because of certain unfavourable reactions which its own boastfulness had produced, partly because, after the World Congress of Churches at Uppsala, it was decided to give itself a mainly ecumenical air. Thus the United Kingdom Editorial Committee of IDO-C became in December 1968 the Pastoral Development Group. But the leading personalities, the President, Father Laurence Bright O.P. of *Slant*, the Catholic-Marxist publication, and his colleagues, were the same; and there is ample evidence of the increased activity of IDO-C here and in many other countries.

The International Committee of IDO-C for the Development of Religious Documentation and Information consists of personalities from the following countries: Africa (none of them Africans), Argentine, Australia, Austria, Belgium, Brazil, Canada, Chile, Colombia, Czechoslovakia, Eire, Finland, France, Germany, Hungary, India, Italy, Lebanon,

Malta, Mexico, the Netherlands, Norway, Peru, Poland, Portugal, Spain, Sweden, Switzerland, the United Kingdom, the United States, Uruguay and Yugoslavia. They are mostly journalists and editors with a sprinkling of professional broadcasters (e.g. Radio Canada, Radio Vatican, Radio Eireann and the Dutch K.R.O.), the most important in the Catholic intellectual field being those representing the *Herder Korrespondenz*, operated by Herder and Herder, who acquired control of Burns and Oates (now defunct) in London and are also prominent in the German and Austrian groups, the *Informations Catholiques Internationales* and the American Catholic 'Establishment' which we have described. Such hitherto respected Catholic reviews as the Jesuit *Civilta Cattolica* in Rome, *Etudes* in Paris and *The Month* in London as well as *The Tablet* and the French *Edition Centurion* are also involved.

It would be easy but tedious to illustrate the uniform style in which such periodicals purvey to their readers news of Catholic happenings in other countries. The following instance will suffice to indicate the standard of reporting. It is from a 'special report from Rome' by Desmond O'Grady an Australian journalist member of IDO-C's International Committee, which appeared in *The Tablet* of 4 April 1970. He refers to a letter by Father Hervé Carrier, Rector of the Pontifical Gregorian University, reproving three professors who had made a statement to the press in favour of allowing divorce in Italy, at a moment when the Pope was known to have taken the opposite position, and to the feelings which this produced in the University.

> 'The reactionaries expressed their sorrow and indignation at the offence to the Pope and assured him of their eternal allegiance. However, the liberals within the conmunity were just as indignant over Fr. Carrier's repressive letter. Several wrote to him in return expressing their shock and dismay . . . His letter was an anathema to those with a belief in academic freedom'.

Observe the meagreness of the progressive's vocabulary.

Anyone who supports the Pope on a moral issue is *ipso facto* a 'reactionary'.

Of more practical importance to the widespread diffusion of IDO-C's notions among the general public are its active members in the secular press, notably Mr. G. Armstrong of *The Guardian*, Mr. M. H. Fesquet of *Le Monde*, the Abbé Laurentin of *Le Figaro*, John Cogley, whom I have already mentioned, of the *New York Times*, Israel Shenker, the Rome correspondent of *Time*, David Meade of the *Chicago Sunday Times*, Dr. Kleine of the *Frankfürter Algemeine* and John Hortan of the *Irish Times*. Nor is there any lack of a supporting cast, to contribute to national newspapers in England.

The two national branches of IDO-C most heavily impregnated with Marxism seem to be the Polish and the British. In Poland it is provided by *Znak*, a 'circle' of Catholics attached to the National Unity Front. Though not an arm of the political police, as is the *Pax* organisation (the Government agency established to undermine loyalty to the hierarchy, so generously publicised by *The Tablet* and French Catholic papers), it is no less opposed to the Primate, Cardinal Wyszynski, and favourable to the Communist system of government. The British section of IDO-C included four leaders of *Slant* and Mr. Jack Dunman, described as a 'specialist in ecumenism', of the Communist Party of Great Britain. It was represented on the central executive committee of IDO-C by Mr. K. N. Middleton of Sheed and Ward, the publisher and editor of *Slant*. Operating on the Left wing of IDO-C in France, though not, I believe, organically connected with it, are the equivalent *Témoignage Chrétien*, *Economie et Humanisme*, *La Lettre*, *Frères du Monde* and *Terre Entière*, which at the time of the students' rebellion in France in the spring of 1968 issued a joint communiqué saying that 'every Christian had a right to share in the revolutionary process including armed action'.

It may well be that the revolutionary Catholic Marxists, led by the wilder Dominicans, are something of an embarrassment to the more respectable members of IDO-C, many of whom are undoubtedly persons of high intellectual and literary merit. All radical movements, however earnest, which set out to undermine existing authority, produce their lunatic fringes. What is far more serious than this kind of extremism, which however is not without influence among the Christian Social clergy of Latin America, is the powerful mechanism of publicity which IDO-C has created in the mass media and especially among the 'quality' newspapers of important countries. Taking account of the facts that we have summarised above, it is no surprise to find every item of news indicative of criticism or defiance of the Papacy and of tradition by Catholic priests, authors, theologians or students, exaggerated and published simultaneously in French, English, American, German, Dutch, Australian and other newspapers. This, as we shall see, is the mechanism which was brought into play to extol Cardinal Suenens' book, *Co-responsibility in the Church*, in May 1968 and his famous 'interview' given to the Informations Catholiques Internationales to revive the campaign for its main thesis[25] a year later.

Besides its effective press service, IDO-C has its own intensive doctrinal action in favour of its self-appointed mission of directing the 'renewal' of the 'Conciliar Church'. It distributes a weekly bulletin in five languages – English, French, German, Italian and Spanish, to bishops, clergy, religious houses, seminaries and journalists all over the world, dealing with the reform of ecclesiastical authority, liturgy, dogma, ethics, ecumenism and so on. The editorial committee which produces this publication includes several of the key personalities who also direct the more high-brow review *Concilium*, which comes out nine times a year, notably Father Schillebeecks, the main author of the Dutch Catechism – the amendment of which by a committee of Cardinals he rejected – and the most intransigent supporter of the revolt of the Dutch Pastoral Council against the Pope on the

---

[1]This is examined in the following chapter.

question of priestly celibacy. Other leading lights on *Concilium*, which is published in eight languages, include Dr. Hans Kung and Charles Davis, the former English priest who left the Church amid so much limelight.

This summary, by no means exhaustive, of the machinery and operations of the rival Catholic 'Establishment', which is equally concerned to advance its own views of the new democratic Church and to suppress information about Catholic movements and publications which oppose them, gives some idea of the uphill task of the Pope in upholding faith and sanity. He has denounced the 'spirit of corrosive criticism which has become fashionable in certain sectors of Catholic life' and, without naming names, has shown by his speech of January 15 1970 that he well knows what IDO-C is about. In particular he warned the faithful against the 'arbitrary intentions' attributed to the Vatican Council and 'the so-called horizontal orientation of religion, directed no longer to the first and supreme love and worship of God, but to the love and worship of man; sociology as the main and determining principle of theological thought and pastoral action; the promotion of an alleged and inconceivable Conciliar Republic; acceptance of the forms and spirit of the Protestant Reformation'. The battle is joined.

# Chapter 9
# Democratisation of the Church

The intellectual leader of the campaign for the democratisation of the Catholic Church is Cardinal Leon-Joseph Suenens, who succeeded the aged Cardinal Van Roey, to whom he had been an Auxiliary, as Primate of Belgium in 1961. He is a man of great charm and volcanic energy, who has an ear to the ground and instinctively picks up the prevailing trends of modern thought. Just as democracy and individual participation in political, social and economic institutions are the order of the day in secular life, so his main preoccupation, as we shall see, is to adapt, or more properly remould, the Universal Church to that image and likeness, on the strength of his interpretation of the 'logic' of the Vatican Council. Apart from this main preoccupation, systematically argued in his book *Coresponsibility in the Church*, published in May 1968, and his much more polemical *Interview* (in fact a campaign programme), launched with more publicity a year later, his main personal enthusiasms are the Third World, and the cultivation of reunion with the Anglican Episcopate. This latter objective seems to him a natural consequence of the famous Malines Conversations between Cardinal Mercier and Lord Halifax at the beginning of the century.

Cardinal Suenens is in consequence known much more as a world figure than as a diocesan bishop. He played a very active part in the Second Vatican Council in which he was soon labelled as one of the 'progressive' leaders: the formulation of episcopal collegiality, the proposed permanent diaconate, an age limit for bishops and the recognition of the charisms bestowed by the Holy Ghost upon the laity were among his main contributions. In 1963 Pope John XXIII sent him to present a copy of his Encyclical *Pacem in terris* to the United Nations.

## The Doctrine of Coresponsibility

The Cardinal devotes the first part of his book to 'The Church Today'. It starts with the statement,

> 'The Second Vatican Council marked the end of an epoch. Or if one wishes to look back even further, it marked the end of a series of epochs. It signified the end of an era. We could say that in a certain way, it closed the age of Constantine, the age of medieval Christianity, the era of the Counter-Reformation, the period of Vatican I. In the context of its ancient past, it marks a turning point in the history of the Church'.

So it is not just a matter of finding contemporary expression for an eternal faith; as John XXIII said in his opening address to the Council,

> 'The substance of the ancient doctrine of the deposit of faith is one thing; the way in which it is presented is another. And it is the latter that must be taken into consideration with patience, if necessary, everything being measured in the forms and proportions of a magisterium which is predominantly pastoral in character."

The author quotes this with approbation, as well as a similar statement by Paul VI after the Council in which he spoke of 'presenting, defending and illustrating the truths of divine faith with ideas and words that are more understandable to minds trained in present-day philosophical and scientific learning'.

But he soon goes far beyond this prudent and minimal conception of the *aggiornamento*, and develops his main thesis, which has much more to do with the distribution of power in the Church than with supernatural faith.

> 'If we were asked what we consider to be the seed of life deriving from the Council which is most fruitful in

> pastoral consequences, we would answer without any hesitation; it is the rediscovery of the people of God as a whole, as a single reality; and then, by way of consequence, the coresponsibility thus implied for every member of the Church'.

He then speaks of the urgency of ecumenism as being one of the principal demands of our times. 'From now on there is a climate of rediscovered brotherhood . . . We await the hour of full communion'. Since the great obstacles that separate Catholics from their non-Catholic brothers are the dogmas of Papal Primacy and Infallibility, these have to be attenuated. As to the first,

> 'Theologians will have to locate the dogma of papal primacy more precisely within the doctrine of collegiality, showing especially, as we have said, that the primacy should be first of all a service'.

As to the second, he quotes the declaration of Bishop Gasser, Secretary for the Commission of the Faith at the First Vatican Council, which defined, and indeed circumscribed the doctrine, in which he showed the Pope, even when speaking *ex cathedra*, to be the spokesman of the body of the faithful as a whole which cannot err in matters of belief.

> 'The unanimous approval expressed by the actual preaching of the whole of the Church's magisterium, united with its Head, is also the rule of faith for pontifical definitions'.

This broadly speaking is obviously acceptable to most thoughtful Catholics, though the behaviour of vagrant and heretical bishops at various stages of the Church's life, including the present, raises a few awkward questions about the inerrancy of the whole Church, unless there is a central, divinely safeguarded authority to pull them together if required. However, here and throughout the Cardinal's work, it is the emphasis that matters; and the emphasis throughout is on bringing the Papacy down more than a peg.

We learn also at the end of this first part of his book,

> 'The Church of Vatican II has but one ambition; to aid the world in freeing men from the bondage of ignorance,

mistrust and fratricidal hatred, and to aid in the building, along with all men of good will, the humanism of tomorrow, combining all the power of the forces of peace'.

One can but wonder what the apostles, the martyrs and saints of 19 centuries would think of this '*one* ambition' even in the social sphere. What of the Kingdom of God? What of supernatural faith? What of holiness? Do they all belong to the era which Vatican II so happily ended?

The rest of Cardinal Suenens' book is devoted to the Coresponsibility of the various human components of the Church. It is a word which is never, oddly enough, properly defined, but which is understood to mean that every baptised person shares responsibility for the organisation and progress of the Christian Church all over the globe. There are chapters on the Coresponsibility of the Papacy, of the Bishops, of Priests, of Theologians, of Deacons, of Religious and of the the laity.

## Church or churches?

In regard to the Papacy, he quotes a number of passages, including part of the *Constitution on the Church* of the recent Council, to the effect that, though individual bishops do not enjoy the prerogative of infallibility, they can nevertheless proclaim Christian doctrine infallibly, provided they maintain the bond of unity among themselves and with Peter's successor. After citing Pope Paul VI's address to four newly consecrated bishops 'The episcopacy is a responsibility, even more a coresponsibility as wide as the world', Cardinal Suenens sums the matter up 'All of these declarations show clearly that, if the primacy is in fact a prerogative of the sovereign pontiff, there can be no question of his governing the Church without the collaboration of the hierarchy'. And his conception of the Christianity of the future, so different from the visible Catholic unity of the past, is well shown in the following passage.

'The more each particular church will be able to develop

> its own spiritual personality, the more the Christian people will mature in a great diversity of rites, theologies (*sic*), disciplines and customs, and the papal primacy will be free to exercise fully its specific roles of assuring the fundamental unity and cohesion of the Church'.

He has a poor view of the College of Cardinals; 68, he says, out of 120 are over 71[26].

> 'Given the determining role of the sacred college in the election of a Pope, it is desirable that a matter so fraught with consequence for the whole people of God be studied by the world synod of bishops and by consultation with the various episcopal conferences'.

In dealing with coresponsibility among the other ranks of the Church, one can but admire the pastoral solicitude and the constant concern for what is practical. There is certainly room for discussion, however, in his conception of the Church not as the universal society, which was the dominant perspective of the *Constitution on the Church*, but as a group of churches each controlled by its particular bishop. 'The universal church is not primarily a society of individuals, nor is it an agglomeration of units joined directly to its head . . . It is a communion of churches which together form the 'Catholic Church'. And he goes on to recommend 'horizontal' collegiality among bishops and between the episcopal conferences, which are now becoming the rule. There is no recognition here of the danger of the local church conforming to the prevailing nationalism or of the needs of those, (and they are legion in these days of swift travel) whose work or leisure takes them into other dioceses and other countries than their own. The more emphasis is given to the diversity of local and national episcopal churches (for though the Cardinal denies the existence of the latter, that is exactly what is now happening, and not only in the Netherlands) 'in the areas of the spiritual, the liturgical, the theological and the pastoral', the more acutely is the division of Catholic unity felt by those who are internationally minded.

---

[26] The Pope's *Motu Proprio* of 23 November 1970, excluding octogenarian Cardinals from the Conclave is a step in the direction which he advocates.

## The Primacy of Community

The main thesis, on which the Suenens doctrine of a Coper-
nican revolution in the Church is based, appears early in
the book which we are considering.

> 'The decision to include within the Constitution on the
> Church a chapter on the people of God sanctioned the
> desire of the Council to derive *all* that ought to be said
> concerning the mission, functions and tasks of the faithful
> from the 'common' or universal Christian condition . . .
> This primacy of baptism entails as an immediate corollary
> the primacy of community. Each one must live and insert
> his personal responsibility in and with that of all the other
> faithful'.

(Surely 'ought to' would be more realistic than 'must',
considering the large number of baptised knaves and fools
in this sinful world). Thus collegiality – the unlovely word
coined to describe the body of bishops enjoying the Apostolic
succession, though never in fact living together as the word
college implies – is to be extended to the whole body of
baptised Christians; a very debatable proposition, surely,
since the promises made to Peter and the mission given to
him and his fellow apostles were clearly confined to that
small body of men appointed to lead, to govern and to teach.
The Cardinal, however, seems to deduce from the radical
equality of all the baptised the idea that these powers have
been given indifferently to all the 'people of God'. When we
come to his chapter on the *Coresponsibility of laymen* he asks
'Is the Church a democracy?' and replies,

> 'The renewal of community in the Church, which ulti-
> mately derives from faith, naturally finds its place within
> the progress of a world moving more and more in the
> direction of democracy. It would seem that as we accentu-
> ate the role of the laity we deny the hierarchical character
> of the Church. But this is not true, provided that we
> understand how the Church accepts democracy within
> herself and the historical context in which, not authority
> itself, but its way of being exercised has come about . . .
> Christ's personality bears the mark of his place and time
> of birth. The Church carries the same marks; as a human
> society it bears the imprints of the time in which it lives . . .

> The Church has seen rule of the type of Constantine, feudal lords and enlightened despots. Today most developed countries have adopted a democratic form of government. All of this pertains to the realm of contingency. It is precisely in this realm that we find a real uneasiness in the Church'.

He refers with sympathy to criticism of the Church's government in recent books and magazines by writers who complain that 'the directing bodies have a way of functioning which is no longer conformed to the atmosphere of our time, as expressed by the spirit and customs with which we are familiar in the civil life of democratic regimes'.

He then points out that in fact elements of monarchy, oligarchy and democracy exist within the Church at the same time in the form of papacy, episcopate and people.

> 'The papal primacy has aspects about it which are monarchical, but the Papacy is unintelligible except as integrated within a universal episcopate and in living connection with the whole body. The episcopacy for its part is not a self-sufficient oligarchy, but reaches out in both directions in a two-fold living relationship: one with its leader, the Pope, and the other with the whole presbyterate and laity . . .'

> 'Having made this reservation, we can now say that the Second Vatican Council certainly was characterised by a move in the direction of "democratisation" because of the accent it placed on the people of God, by the stress it laid on the hierarchy as a service and by its creation of certain organisms within the Church which favour democratic methods of government'.

## Some doubts about Democracy

There is much that is edifying and thought-provoking in Cardinal Suenens' book. If we have concentrated upon the parts affecting the distribution of powers in the Church, it is because these have been seized upon most eagerly by all those writers and publicists, whose organisation we studied in the last chapter and whose main interest is to diminish Papal authority and especially to contest the Pope's right to give binding judgments on matters affecting sexual morality and the tradition of faith. Before proceeding to examine the way in which the Cardinal was tempted, or inclined, to play up to that chorus a year later, it is permissible to ask whether 'democracy' is after all a good model to which the structure of the Church should be made to conform at the present stage of history. There are a great many kinds of democracy in vogue, from the People's Democracies in which a single party imposes its will upon the well-drilled proletariat, to the democracy of the new states of Africa and Asia which, with hardly a single exception, has yielded in the space of a few months or years either to the dictatorship of a single man or party or, as in the case of India, to chronic disorder. In most of the Western World the feuds of political parties, even if incorrupt, have not contributed to a high sense of civic unity or moral respect for the state; and in the principal home of this political doctrine, the United States, as in France and Italy, democratic institutions are on trial, since it is an open question how far they can contain the new forms of revolution against authority. We may certainly agree that, given a sound constitutional framework, the parliamentary system in which all have the right to vote – though a large number never do – is a tolerable safeguard against injustice or despotism in Western society. It does not necessarily follow that this imperfect system, recently evolved to meet the needs of temporal politics in this vale of tears, is a good one for a world-wide spiritual society whose principle of unity is supernatural, as the Catholic Church has always been held to be. Cardinal Suenens allows that the creed cannot be drawn up by a democratic majority. It is equally true that the inerrancy of a single authority safeguarding the one faith is, odd as it may seem, less incredible to millions of Catholics than the simultaneous infallibility of 2,800 bishops scattered all over the world, which is what collegiality in its extreme form really amounts to. Obviously Pope and Bishops should normally be at one in exercising the Church's *magisterium*. But if they are *not*, as recent painful examples of dissension about the regulation of births, priestly celibacy or the contents of catechisms have shown – and the proposed impact of local democracy upon the election of bishops and their pastoral duties will increase the danger – the only secure life-line for the average Catholic priest or layman is his dependence upon the word of the Pope.

## The Manifesto

Thanks to the efficient journalistic machinery of IDOC, a long manifesto described as an Interview given by Cardinal Suenens to Mr. José de Broucker, editor of the *Informations Catholiques Internationales*, was published in that review on 15 May 1969. Mr. St. John Stevas, M.P., introduced it as 'a blockbuster' in *The Times*; *Le Monde* gave a whole page to it. It was published simultaneously *in toto* in diverse languages in *The Tablet* (London) on 17 May; the *National Catholic Reporter* (Kansas City), *Orientierung* (Zurich), *Internationale Kathoolike Informatie* (Bruges), *Informationês Catolicas Internacionales* (Mexico), *Famiglia Mese* (Milan), *Glas Concilia* (Zagreb), *Via* (Prague), *Tygodnik Powszechruy*, the organ of *Znak* (Cracow) and in *Vigilia* (Budapest). It was a highly organised operation[27]. This document, described as answers to various questions raised about points in the book *Co-responsibility in the Church*, is sharper in tone than the original work and more openly critical of any Papal action unless undertaken in consultation with the episcopate as a whole. The reason for this is not far to seek. It was after the book was written that Pope Paul's Encyclical *Humanae Vitae* was issued in which, contrary to the advice of a majority of his consultative commission, he had maintained the traditional teaching of the Church against artificial means of contraception. Cardinal Suenens, who had chaired a number of conferences on birth control, was extremely critical of this document which, it will be recalled, caused an

---

[27]The same technique was used for the next annual pronouncement of the Cardinal in May 1970 in favour of open discussion between Bishops and priests of the 'question' of celibacy.

outcry in the secular press and more especially in the publications associated with IDOC.

The following quotations from the 'Interview' illustrate the author's convictions.

### The Pope and the Bishops

'It is important to avoid presenting the role of the Pope in such a way as to isolate him from the college of bishops whose leader he is. While we emphasise that the Pope has a right to act or speak alone, the world "alone" never means "separately" or "in isolation".

'It is impossible to over-emphasise the vital unity of the apostolic college. The divine help promised to Peter and his successors does not take the form of a personal inspiration from God but of special help in the normal working out of collegiality'.

'It follows the logic of Vatican II that the individual churches, through their bishops gathered in episcopal conferences, should be consulted publicly and collectively, and enabled to collaborate in documents that vitally affect the whole Church. And that, not merely by associating their strictly theological commissions in the work, but also be including lay people qualified to speak on the matter at issue'.

### The Election of Bishops, Cardinals and Pope

'The idea has been put forward in various places that the laity too should be associated in the election of a Pope. Apart from the fact that it seems hard to see how such a thing could be practicable, it seems to me that the solution which would come closest to this legitimate desire would be to associate the laity more closely with the election of bishops. The bishops would then be, not just theologically but psychologically, more recognisable as spokesmen for the people while still remaining their leaders'.

How then can popularly elected bishops play their part in electing the Pope? The Cardinals, in the existing law of the Church, form an electoral college for the purpose: but Cardinals are appointed by the Pope, and this must stop. Here Cardinal Suenens is most outspoken, in contending that the break with the past intended by Vatican II involves a change of *regime* as real as that resulting from the Revolutions of 1789 and 1917.

> 'In the past, kings used to administer the state however they chose. Even those who did not say, *l'Etat c'est moi*, as Louis XIV is said to have done, raised armies, minted money, decreed taxes, and conferred benefices and titles on anyone they pleased. All that is over, and such things are decided now with the help of a mandate given by popular elections. In the Church we have not yet completed the change of régime'.

> 'We witness an uneasiness, a sense of dislocation from our age, every time a "promotion" to the Cardinalate is announced . . . It is a form of solitary decision whose objective criteria cannot be known and about which dialogue is not possible. No one denies the legality of the procedure. The only question is whether this age-old custom is in line with collegiality, in the spirit of Vatican II or not . . . Anything that arouses a suspicion of favouritism, of the good pleasure of the Prince, is a harking back to the days of absolute monarchies and a source of uneasiness'.

The author concludes, therefore, that Cardinals should be chosen by episcopal conferences, the Pope ratifying their choice. Having then provided for the more or less democratic election of bishops and cardinals, how could the same principle be applied to the election of the Pope?

> 'Should the electoral college be, in the first place, the whole body of bishops, and then as a second step, a narrower college of bishops, or should recourse be made to the synod of Bishops[28] and, if so, what form should that synod take? . . . the whole concept of the Church would be falsified if one declared that this question concerned the Pope alone, and not the members of the Church'.

## Legalism and Life

A note of demagogy creeps into the contrasts which the Cardinal constantly draws in this manifesto between the exuberant life, inspired by the Holy Ghost, which he professes to see in the 'periphery' of the Church, that is in the

---

[28] It now has a permanent secretariat in Rome.

local 'Churches', and the legalism of the Holy See at the centre,

> 'At the centre, the prevailing tendency is still strongly marked by a formalist, juridicial vision of things . . . an existentialist, bureaucratic, static, juridical, centralising tendency'.
>
> 'The centre is blocking development . . . It does not believe in the coresponsibility of the bishops – and Vatican II has not yet been translated into life on the level of collegiality. This is a tragic situation which is holding back the pastoral advance of the post-Conciliar period and intensifying the tendency of protesters'.
>
> 'We must look first, not to any code of canon law, however venerable it may be, but to the Gospels and the Acts of the Apostles which immerse us directly in the mystery of Pentecost. Any worthwhile discussion we have can only begin from there'.

This appeal of private judgment direct to scripture without any regard to the tradition of the Church is pure Protestantism and can be respected as such. But it is completely at variance with the whole spirit of the Roman Catholic Church as it has developed and as, *pace* Cardinal Suenens, it was reaffirmed, though in new terms, by the Ecumenical Council. There are many, like Bishop Butler in England, who welcome the Cardinal's gospel and indeed he has evolved the most logical scheme for democratising and thereby revolutionising the Universal Church. We have given these extracts from his writings at some length, because they evidently provide an aura of intellectual respectability for the lesser anti-Papal propagandists and innovators of the day and so contribute most seriously to the prevailing confusion in the Catholic Church. They also face the convinced Catholic with a stark alternative. If the Cardinal is right in claiming that the Popes who have made important decisions without the massive consultation and consent of the world's Bishops, have been acting *ultra vires*, then practically all the papal judgments of past centuries are worthless. If, however, one accepts the personal nature of Christ's mandates to Peter, 'Thou' (not you all collectively) 'art Peter and upon this rock I will build my church', 'Feed my sheep', 'Confirm thy brethren', one is bound, ultimately to uphold the monarchical as against the popular source of Church authority and to accept the Pope's ruling upon what is and what is not meant by the Council on this subject.

> 'They would be mistaken, therefore', Pope Paul said at a general audience in January 1966, 'who might think that the Council represents a severance, or break, or, as some believe, a liberation from the traditional teaching of the Church'.

And in February 1968 he declared, in advance of Cardinal Suenens' thesis,

> 'The Church is hierarchical. It is not amorphous. It is not democratic, in the sense that no one has priority in matters of faith and doctrine over the one whom the Holy Spirit has placed as head of the Church of God'.

It is difficult, in view of this, to see how the democratic campaign of the Belgian Primate can be pursued without precipitating a serious collision, friendly as are his personal relations with Paul VI.

# Chapter 10
# The New Theology

'. . . a time when the clear, fixed stars of the Catholic faith are momentarily obscured by theological smog'. Cardinal John Wright [29].

The intellectual disturbance of the Catholic world since the Vatican Council is very largely the consequence of the conflict between what is described as the 'new theology' and the traditional Christian doctrines of faith and ethics. Pope Paul VI, insisting that the latter were not changed by the Council, of which he is the authoritative interpreter, finds his pronouncements under constant attack from the so-called new theologians, mainly German, Dutch and French with supporting voices in the United States, Italy, England and other Western countries, who claim to speak for the post-Conciliar church.

The new theology is difficult to define, though its practical effects are only too clear. There are evidently two inter-locking trends; one an interpretative philosophy of the evolution of the world, including human society in the light of modern science, which is the consequence of theories, which have been in ferment for half a century at least; the other, the demagogic tendency to provide theoretic justification for the revolt against authority, in accordance with the prevailing gospel of democracy and the loosening of moral standards in contemporary society.

---

²⁹In his foreword to Cardinal Garrone's book *This we believe*.

A further general characteristic of this powerful movement, which distinguishes its leaders from those, both of the Protestant Reformation of the 16th century and of the Enlightenment in the 18th, who repudiated Roman Catholicism, is the resolve of its exponents to remain within and use the world-wide organisation of the Catholic Church. In this they have an advantage at present in the prudence of Pope Paul VI, who, though he is constantly decrying the errors propounded, is resolved, almost to the point of obsession, not himself to be responsible for a schism. The unhappy price of this reticence, in the short run, is that thousands of the faithful and their children are left at the mercy of priests and professors who preach and teach notions even more dissolvent of the Faith than the heresies of an earlier age or the modernism so firmly condemned in the Encyclical *Pascendi domini gregis* of St. Pius X 63 years ago. It may be argued that, in the long run, this policy will be vindicated, by allowing time for the excesses of the moment, such as the clamour against priestly celibacy, to wear themselves out or be overcome by sweet reason, without the lasting consequences of the local or national rupture with Rome which characterised the revolt four centuries ago. The Pope's cautious rallying of support from the bulk of the Catholic hierarchies of the world for his position on celibacy, through the enquiries which he caused his Secretary of State, Cardinal Villot to undertake, rather than risk a head-on collision with the Church in the Netherlands, is cited in support of this view. We are here concerned, however, with the substance of the new teachings rather than with tactics.

Let us start with original sin. How anyone who has observed the course of international politics during the present century can doubt the existence and power of the evil propensities of the human race, passes comprehension. It is the one inescapable fact. It is defined fairly enough in the old penny catechism as 'dimness of intellect, weakness of will and inclination towards evil'.

## Original Sin

'Does anyone preach about original sin any more?' asks Cardinal Garrone[30]. 'Here is another truth we no longer dare to face. We have to admit that it is not easy to picture the concrete conditions that surrounded original sin. The familiar landscape of the Book of Genesis is continually being overcast by nebulous mists in which science hides the infinitely remote past of the human race'.

Yet he goes on to recall that original sin is a tenet of our faith. 'On this point perhaps more than any other, it is necessary to hold to the Church's teaching. For is it not, as Pascal said, the mystery apart from which everything else becomes a mystery to us?'

The essential doctrine, scriptural images apart, is that the hereditary defects and evil propensities in man are to be traced to the misuse of their free will by our first parents – however remote they were in the evolution of the created universe – in disobeying their Creator.

> 'All of us have suffered a deprivation, a separation from God, an increased propensity to unbalance and evil that must be called a Sin because of its origin and nature. Christ delivered us in principle by his death, and he will continue to deliver each of us individually until the end of of time. In Adam we were sinners; in Christ, the new Adam, we are called to liberty and justice'.

This doctrine of original sin, '*quae tantum et talem meruit habere Redemptorem*', is the first and most obvious victim of the theory of evolution. But even more practically damaging to the standard of human behaviour is, as we shall see, the effect of the philosophy of a particularly powerful Catholic apostle of evolution upon the objective reality of actual, that is, personal sin. 'To sin', writes Cardinal Garrone,

> 'is to break the rapport of truth that should exist between the Creator and his creature, between the Father and his child. Sin is committed on the level of a personal relationship; and the two persons confronting each other are not two human beings but the Creator and a creature made in his own likeness, called to a life of union with him'.

---

30In *This we Believe*.

This is the basis for the moral discipline of the Church and its sacramental system by which grace is given to remit and to avoid sin. Because each sin of thought, word, deed or omission is regarded as a personal offence against God, it is necessary to repent of it and, if it be a mortal, that is really deliberate, sin, to confess and be absolved from it in order to regain a state of grace, that is union with God. Hence frequent auricular confession has been recommended and became a regular part of the practising Catholic's life.

## The Decline of Confession

What do we find now? A great decrease in the number of confessions and the explaining away by modern theologians of what constitutes a sin especially in the sexual sphere. Thus we read in the report of a congress of three hundred moral theologians from Italian seminaries and ecclesiastical faculties held at Padua in March 1970[31] the conclusion that 'the individual conscience is the Christian's supreme authority above the papal magisterium, in spheres where dogma is not involved'. Father Bernard Hearing, a German theologian, declared that it was absurd of conservative theologians, for instance, to hold that married couples were acting against the Church if they followed their consciences and had recourse to artificial methods of contraception in opposition to papal teaching. The congress then, we read, discussed 'the urgent need for a reform of confession'. A Hungarian Jesuit, teaching at the Gregorian University, spoke of the decline in the number of confessions and the related decrease in the number of communions, and suggested replacing the discipline of the confessional with 'joint absolution of the faithful' during the act of penitence at the beginning of the Mass; an easy, but practically worthless way out.

This striking falling off in recourse to the sacrament of penance, which is reported from many parts of the Western world, may seem of no great significance to the non-Catholic

---

[31] Reported in *The Tablet*, 11 April 1970.

reader; but, to those acquainted with the rhythm of a healthy Catholic sacramental life, it is a disturbingly true barometer of the sense of personal responsibility for keeping, or not keeping, the will of God. It is not likely that in a year or two Catholics as a whole have suddenly become less sinful. It is much more probable that the sense of sin has diminished. Why is that? It is not only because, as Cardinal Garrone writes, it is no longer fashionable to preach about sin. It is that a school of thought, prevalent in the new theology and consequently permeating Catholic catechetical activities and education, has for some time been at work to *depersonalize* sin – apart from the loosening of sexual morality – and to make relative, and not absolute, the terms within which good and evil are defined.

## The philosophy of Teilhard de Chardin

It is here that the influence of the late Father Teilhard de Chardin has been so decisive. His major works have had an immense appeal, and especially his masterpiece, the *Phenomenon of Man*, written between 1938 and 1940 in Peking, where he was working as Scientific Adviser to the Geological Survey of China, the outbreak of the war having prevented his return to France. He added a preface in 1947 and, in 1948, in Rome, a short appendix on the Place and Part of Evil in a World in Evolution. The complete work was published in English in 1959 four years after his death. The great fascination of this work is that it seems to offer a complete scientific explanation of life from its earliest and simplest appearance in the world right up to contemporary society and beyond, as 'one gigantic process', to quote Sir Julian Huxley, 'a process of becoming, of attaining new levels of existence and organisation, which can properly be called a genesis or an evolution'. Further, for minds disturbed by a supposed conflict of science and religion Teilhard offered a 'Christianisation of evolution' when, after describing the phenomenon of man as one of many scientific phenomena, though the highest of them, he introduces 'the Christian phenomenon', for,

> 'Neither in the play of its elemental activities which can only be set in motion by the hope of an "imperishable", nor in the play of its collective affinities, which require for their coalescence the action of conquering love, can reflective life continue to function and to progress unless, above it, there is a pole which is supreme in attraction and consistence . . . Christ, principle of universal vitality, because sprung up as man among men, put himself in the position (maintained ever since) to subdue unto himself, to purify, to direct and superanimate the general ascent of consciousness into which he inserted himself. By a perennial act of communion and sublimation, he aggregates to himself the total psychism of the earth. And when he has gathered everything together and transformed everything he will close in upon himself and his conquests, thereby rejoining in a final gesture the divine focus he has never left'.

## Teilhardism and free will

This is as noble as it is lyrical, though not easy to understand, any more than the first chapter of St. John's Gospel or the 'Alpha and Omega' of his Apocalypse, with which Père Teilhard de Chardin's vision seems, for all its sublimated generalisation, to correspond. It is not, however, in this sense that his influence has had such a dissolvent effect upon Catholic doctrine. It is in its bearing upon the free will of individual human beings with whose personal guidance and salvation the Church is first of all concerned. Even if the evolution of the physical universe, as Teilhard traces it, were an historical certainty – which it clearly can never be, though it is the accepted probability – the idea that it extends to the moral order is neither proved nor probable. The whole of the Christian doctrine of Redemption ultimately depends upon the personal responsibility of each human soul – beginning with the first – and his liberty to obey or disobey the will of God; which brings us back to the fact of sin and, on the other hand, to the positive virtues which it is possible for a human being to exercise. But human responsibility, with all its unpredictable applications, is wholly destroyed if men are taught to believe that they are simply part of an inevitable process of evolution, like the fatalism of Marx's economic determinism. It is also intrinsic to this single overriding explanation that this process, assimilated to the development of living organisms from lower to higher forms, implies an equally inevitable *progress* to a better state of society, a higher unity (an idea which the course of recent history wholly belies), not to speak of a new universal religion for the evolving universe. It is this will-o'-the wisp of inevitable progress, in which, as we see from Teilhard's own attitude, the ruling authority of the Church is of little consequence, that has bewitched the new theology. Let us confront his conception of the place of evil in the world with the personal conception of sin defined above. 'The problem of evil' he wrote[32] 'no longer exists in our modern perspectives of a Universe in a stage of cosmogenesis'. The creative action of God, in his view, consists continually in 'unifying the multiple' – which apparently means the material and spiritual universe in all its complexity. And the multiple 'because it is the multiple, that is essentially subject to the play of chance in its arrangements . . . cannot possibly progress towards unity without engendering evil by a *statistical necessity*'. As for original sin 'fundamentally our Universe has always been (as any conceivable Universe must be) in its totality and since its origins, a mixture of good and evil fortunes (*chances*); that is to say, impregnated with evil; that is, in a state of original sin; that is, baptisable[33]'. Where, one may ask, does individual free will come into the picture?

## Relativity of Christianity
In another place[34] Teilhard writes 'all those notions transposed into the dimensions of cosmogenesis become clear

[32]Comment je vois.
[33]Letter of 19 June 1953.
[34]1 January 1951.

and cohere in an astounding way'. And what are those notions? He eunmerates them 'Creation, Spirit, Evil, God – and especially Original Sin, Cross, Resurrection, Parousia, Charity'. So much for the historic Christianity in which, contradictory as it may seem, he professed to believe to the end; (this must have been the case, for each half of a schizophrenic mind can be in itself genuine). But for people of normal intelligence, whether Christian or not, it is obvious that Teilhard reduces to a purely relative status the facts, events and persons which have absolute value in the Catholic tradition. And on the Moral Law he is obscure.

This is the consequence of his absorbing passion with the theory of evolution. Fascinated with stones from his childhood, he became a brilliant palaeantologist and biologist, and was steeped in the advances of modern science. For him the world in evolution became the overriding force and explanation of all things. So it was for his friend Sir Julian Huxley and others undisturbed by a Catholic conscience. What distinguished Teilhard from his non-Catholic contemporaries was his attempt to conciliate the Catholic Christianity of his upbringing and his priestly calling with this newly discovered enthusiasm for the evolving world, because the Catholic faith 'rooted in the notion of the Incarnation, has always in its structure attached great importance to the tangible values of the World and matter[35].' So he called for 'a new Christology stretched to the organic dimensions of our new universe'.

But which is the more important. Jesus Christ or Evolution? Religion or Progress? God or the World? It is in the priority given by Teilhard de Chardin to the latter of these alternatives that lies his great aberration and his main danger to the theologians and philosophers who have been fascinated by his writings. Thus in his *Comment je crois* we read,

> 'If by consequence of some internal upheaval I came to lose successively my faith in Christ, my faith in a personal

God, my faith in the Spirit, it seems to me that I should continue to believe in the World. The World (the value, the infallibility and the goodness of the World) such in the final analysis is the first and only thing in which I believe. It is by this faith that I live, and it is to this faith, I feel, that at the moment of dying I shall, above all doubts, abandon myself . . . To this confused faith in a World, One and infallible, I abandon myself, wherever it may lead me'.[36]

Yet despite this unbalanced apotheosis of a personified World (so far removed from the more ugly world of wars, massacres and collective hatreds in which we live), Teilhard did not lose his faith in Christ. He transformed Him in his mind into the 'Omega-Christ', Omega being in his philosophy, the culminating point of the evolutionary process, and saw Him, since His mission as the Redeemer had become obscured by the evaporation of original sin, as the motive-power and end-product of evolution. In this perspective the existing doctrines of Christianity would have to be reshaped or thrown overboard in order to arrive at the desired synthesis,

'I have come to the conclusion that, in order to pay for a drastic revalorisation and amorisation of the substance of things, a whole series of reshaping of certain representations or attitudes, which seem to us definitely fixed by Catholic dogma, has become necessary if we sincerely wish to *Christify Evolution*. Seen thus, and because of ineluctable necessity, one could say that a hitherto unknown form of religion (a religion hitherto unimaginable and indescribable, since until now the Universe has not been large enough to contain it) is gradually germinating in the heart of modern Man in the furrow opened by the idea of Evolution'.[37]

## Relations with Rome

It is not surprising that from 1924 onward Father Teilhard de Chardin had been in trouble with Rome. As he told Fr. Auguste Valensin in that year, 'I have got off with the

---

[36] *Comment je crois* quoted in *Pensée philosophique et religieuse du Père Teilhard de Chardin*, by Dom Georges Frenaud, Monk of Solesmes.
[37] *The Stuff of the Universe*.

comment that I am heretical or that I "have a screw loose". This was about original sin; but powerful Jesuit protection saved him from immediate trouble, once the General of the Society, Father Ledochowski, had persuaded him to sign a text describing the doctrine on this subject in traditional terms. This led, however, to the long prohibition of his superiors to publish philosophical books, with the result that it was only after his death that his major works appeared. As he accumulated a vast body of followers, as well as a less vocal body of critics, the Holy See evidently became disturbed at his evolutionary progressivism, and Pius XII's Encyclical *Humani Generis* of August 1950 was generally believed to be directed against him. Long after his death the Congregation of the Holy Office issued in June 1962 a belated warning (*Monitum*) to all Ordinaries, Superiors of Religious Institutes, Rectors of Seminaries and Principals of Universities, exhorting them 'to safeguard the minds, especially of the young, against the dangers of the works of Father Teilhard de Chardin and of his supporters', because 'Leaving aside any judgment in so far as the positive sciences are concerned, it is sufficiently manifest that in the matter of philosophy and theology the aforementioned works are full of such ambiguities, or rather grave errors, as to offend Catholic doctrine'. This was on the eve of the convening of the Vatican Council; and it simply acted as a stimulus to the modernists and progressives to accept and propound Teilhard's ideas, since the Holy Office had become their particular Aunt Sally, the embodiment of the reactionary Roman Curia.

All this makes it the more astonishing that Teilhard de Chardin decided to the last to remain within the fold of the Roman Church. His reason for doing so is of great importance and goes far to explain why the new theologians, whom he has inspired, have decided to follow his example rather than take the more downright – and one would have thought more honest – decision of earlier reformers to break loose. This reason emerges from a letter written by Teilhard on 4 October 1950, printed in *Le Concile et Teilhard, l'Eternel et l'Humain* published in Switzerland in 1963 and reproduced more recently with a commentary by Henri Rambaud. A few weeks after the appearance of the Encyclical *Humani Generis* a certain Father G. who had left the Dominican Order and the Church, wrote to him 'guessing his difficulties' and suggested that he should follow his example and join, with him, the 'Old Catholics', who since the First Vatican Council had rejected papal infallibility. In his reply Teilhard agreed that the Church needed change and reformation. It must be a 'reformation not only of institutions and morals but of faith'. What was required was 'a new faith for the world – faith in what is above (*l'en Haut*) combined with a faith in progress (*l'en Avant*), and I believe that only Christianity can do it'.

> 'That being so (and it is here that we differ . . .), I still do not see any better means of bringing about what I anticipate myself than to work towards the reformation (as defined above) *from within*: that is by remaining sincerely attached to the *phylum*[38], whose development I expect to see. In all sincerity (and without wishing to criticise the step you have taken) I find that only the Roman stem, taken in its entirety, can provide a biological transformation to which I look forward. And this is not pure speculation. In the last 50 years I have watched the revitalisation of Christian thought and life taking place around me – in spite of every Encyclical – too closely not to have an unbounded confidence in the power of the old Roman stem to reanimate itself. Let us each work in our own way. All upward movements converge'.

## Influence on the New Theology

It seems evident that, in its *weltanschauung*, Father Teilhard de Chardin, though himself only a theologian *per accidens*, is the father of the New Theology. Every one of the major tendencies which we observe today, except the common

---

[38]Defined in the Concise Oxford Dictionary as a 'division of the animal kingdom containing classes of animals'. For examples vertebrates form a phylum within the animal kingdom.

toadying to the prevailing sexual obsession and to democracy for which we have discerned other origins, is to be found in his writings which we have quoted. There is the almost idolatrous belief in progress. There is the notion that evolution is the secret of the universe and that traditional Christian doctrine must be trimmed or developed to fit it. There is in consequence the emphasis on 'becoming' rather than 'being'. This, and the notion of sin as simply one of the elements which inevitably make up the complex universe as a statistical necessity, operate against the direct moral relationship of each man, woman and child with God. There is the mission to achieve a new world religion free from the fetters of the old. There is the superior contempt of the *illuminati*, who imagine that they have this mission, for the teaching and ruling functions of the Church's magisterium, Papal pronouncements included. This, of course, is sufficient to ensure the new theologians' instinctive opposition to any papal action which they do not feel conforms with their own libertarian and democratic interpretation of the recent Council's documents. Yet this prevailing *hubris* does not reduce the determination of these intellectuals to remain within the framework of the Roman Catholic Church and to make the fullest use of its organisation, loyalties, and facilities for their own ends, precisely for the practical reason given by Teilhard in his letter. I do not suggest for a moment that some of the prophets of the new theology – though certainly not all – are not men of the highest learning and ability, like the Jesuit theologian Father Rahner, and of course there are many variations of moderation or extremism and many points of debate among them – as can be seen from any number of *Concilium*. But the main characteristics of Teilhardism, reinforced by the opportunities for innovation provided by the Vatican Council, stand out a mile.

## The New Theology in Action

If we look for practical consequences, nothing is more revealing than the effrontery of the following passage from a recent article[39] of that militant of the new theologians' trade-union, Dr. Hans Kung. He is referring to the Papal *Motu proprio* of May 1970 relaxing the rules about mixed marriages.

> 'The attenuation of ecclesiastical authority continues. After questionable decisions on birth control, celibacy and civil divorce, after various attempts to restore a pre-conciliar theology (examples of which are the Encyclical on the Eucharist, the papal Credo, the moves against the Dutch Catechism) and a Roman 'ecumenism'' restricted to gestures and visits, comes the new *Motu Proprio* on mixed marriages; a development surprising only to those who were still expecting serious steps to be taken during this pontificate towards ecclesiastical renewal and ecumenical understanding'.

These offensive references to papal teaching and decisions are typical of the so-called new theology. The disparagement of Pope Paul VI's *Credo of the people of God* is particularly serious, for the Pope claimed his full authority in enunciating this exposition of the Nicene Creed and other basic tenets of the faith, in full agreement with declarations of the Council and with the wishes of the Synod of bishops of 1968. So too is the recent ruling, the *Motu Proprio* on mixed marriages in accordance with the views of the more recent Synod of 1969, as the West German Bishops' Conference pointed out in reproving Kung for his polemical and offensive article, saying that 'the final draft had the complete agreement of the various bishops' conferences'[40]. One wonders how much longer this turbulent priest, who has however a great following, can continue to call himself a Catholic, for he goes on to write in his article 'modern theology disputes how far marriage may be called a sacrament at all by comparison with baptism or the Eucharist'.

It will be clear from this chapter that it is the very substance of the Catholic faith which is being continuously and diligently undermined by this *trahison des clercs*.

---

[39] In *The Tablet*, 30 May 1970.
[40] *The Tablet*, 6 June 1970.

## PART FIVE

# Ecumenism and Politics

# Chapter 11

# Principles, and reconciliation with the East

## General tenor of the Council's Decree

'Reunion all round' was one of Ronald Knox's most entertaining satirical pamphlets (*c.* 1914), when the idea of corporate Christian reunion was an exclusively Liberal Protestant idea and could be viewed as a form of idealized indifferentism. Nobody then seriously considered that the Roman Catholic Church, claiming as it did to be the one true Church of Christ, with the divinely instituted papal authority and a validly ordained ministry to offer the sacrifice of the Mass and administer the sacraments, could be involved in that process. It is a measure of the dramatic change which the initiative of John XXIII has effected, that it should now be the Roman Church itself which has become the principal animator of the movement for the reunion of Christendom. Indeed, not content with aiming at the unity of Christians to fulfil the prayer of the Lord 'That they may all be one' (John 17.21), the Vatican Council reached out for an understanding with non-Christian religions, Moslems and Jews in particular, and established a secretariat for dialogue with unbelievers. It is this latter operation, going far beyond the limits of inter-Christian discussion, which has been seized upon by avant-garde enthusiasts and self-appointed interpreters of post-Conciliar Catholicism to entangle themselves and their students in Communist propaganda under the general title of ecumenism, with the most compromising results.

So we are faced here, as in many fields, with the authentic

principles enunciated by the Council and, on the other hand, with the way in which they are used and exploited for dubious purposes. And human nature being what it is, the danger overhanging all open-ended dialogue and co-operation between a Church, whose whole *raison d'etre* is to be the sure depository of divine truth, and organisations whether religious or ideological which reject that claim, is inevitably the tendency to play down real intellectual differences in the interests of agreement or at least a *modus vivendi*. I believe that it is precisely because the ordinary layman, Catholic, Anglican or Protestant feels this to be a dishonest proceeding that, despite the fervour of small minorities, there is as yet so little lay support in this country for a movement which, on the face of it, is such an admirable espression of Christian charity and in which the Vatican Council urged all Catholics to take part.

It is necessary, before facing some disturbing by-products of the movement, to understand the Council's real intentions. The Decree on Ecumenism, drafted by Cardinal Bea and his Unity Secretariat, begins by recalling the insistence, revealed in so many texts of Christ himself and His Apostles, upon the unity of the Church which he founded. It was built upon Peter to whom 'he promised the keys of the kingdom of heaven'; yet the meaning of this is, of course, precisely the subject of dissent between the Roman Church and the churches and 'ecclesial communities' which have separated themselves from it.

> 'From the beginning divisions have appeared in this Church which is one and unique . . . Succeeding ages have seen the birth of greater quarrels, and communities of considerable size have broken away from full fellowship in the Catholic Church. The fault has sometimes been on both sides . . . Men who believe in Christ and who have duly received baptism are established in a fellowship with the Catholic Church, even if the fellowship be incomplete. There are various real points of disagreement between them and the Catholic Church on matters of doctrine and discipline and on the question of the Church's structural

organisation. These disagreements provide many impediments and, in some cases, serious obstacles in the way of full fellowship with the Church. It is the aim of the ecumenical movement to surmount these obstructions'.

Among the recommended characteristics of this movement are: efforts to do away with any terms or decisions that do not fairly correspond to the position of the separated brethren; 'dialogue between competent experts at meetings of Christians of different churches and communities'; and fuller collaboration in fulfilling social duties for the common good. 'This is the road that leads, over the obstacles, to complete communion, to the gathering of all Christians at a single celebration of the Eucharist in the unity of the one and only Church'.

This is indeed, a high ideal, one visible communion for all, a very different conception from 'inter-communion' between Churches retaining various differences from one another, a preliminary stage which cannot itself be attained without agreement upon the basic significance of the sacrament and upon the authority of those charged with its celebration. So far the rule *nulla communicatio in sacris* – an honest rule, it must be said, which was respected and understood as much by an Evangelical clergyman, like my father, as by Catholics – has obtained, preventing common services between Roman Catholics and Protestants. This rule is now waived on the Catholic side by the Council, except for the vital matter of Holy Communion.

> 'In certain certain circumstances such as the appointed prayers "for unity", and ecumenical meetings, the association of Catholics in prayers with their separated brethren is not only lawful but desirable. Such prayers in common are a very effective means of winning the grace of unity . . . Sharing in sacred rites, however is not to be applied indiscriminately as a means to the reunion of Christians. Sharing of this kind is based on two principles: expression of unity of the Church and sharing of the means of grace. Expression of unity excludes sharing for the most part. The grace to be won sometimes recommends it'.

It is left to Bishops 'to make a prudent decision with reference to circumstances of time, place and person'.

We then have the principles to govern organised dialogue,

> 'Properly prepared Catholics should improve their knowledge of their brethrens' particular teaching and history, spiritual and liturgical life, religious psychology and culture. Meetings of the two sides are a great help to this end, especially when their purpose is the discussion of theological questions on a basis of equality, provided that those taking part, with the bishops keeping watch, are real experts'.

This is the kind of dialogue which has since been organised in a most serious manner between learned clerics of the Roman and other churches, notably the joint meetings of the Anglican-Roman Catholic commission in which Bishop Butler, himself a former Anglican, has taken such a leading part. The Decree lays down an important proviso,

> 'The method of presenting Catholic belief should prove no obstacle to dialogue with the brethren. What is absolutely necessary is that the whole teaching be expressed with lucidity. Nothing is so foreign to ecumenism as the false attitude of appeasement which is damaging to the purity of Catholic doctrine and obscures its genuine, established meaning'.

A section is devoted to education and to the training of clergy, beginning 'The teaching of sacred theology and other subjects, especially history, should be treated from an ecumenical viewpoint, so that their correspondence to reality may be increasingly exact'. This has already led to the amalgamation of a number of Catholic colleges and theological faculties in secular universities, joint Catholic-Protestant seminaries and the like, especially in the United States. Detailed effect was given to the Council's Decree by the Secretariat of Christian Unity in Rome in April 1970 in the second part of its Directory on Ecumenism, dealing with Higher Education in general and with the Ecumenical Dimension of Religious and Theological Education. A quotation from the latter will illustrate the new spirit prevailing.

'To give adequate emphasis to the Catholic and apostolic character of the Church, the Ecumenical spiritual life of Catholics should also be nourished from the treasures of many traditions, past and present, which are alive in other Churches and ecclesial communities; such are the treasures found in the liturgy, monasticism and mystical tradition of the Christian East; in Anglican worship and piety; in the evangelical prayer and spirituality of Protestants'.

## Overture to the Eastern Churches

Before considering how this radical change in attitude of the Catholic Church is working out in practice in the Western World in which we live, let us look at the Council's hopes and proposals for reunion between the Roman See and the Eastern Orthodox Churches, an entirely different question from that involved in the attempt to mend the rift resulting from the Protestant Reformation of the 16th century.

In its section on Eastern Churches the ecumenical decree of the Council has nothing but praise for the faith, liturgy and sacramental life of these Churches and their particular local character which there is not the least desire to change. The period before the schism which divided East and West is nostalgically recalled 'It was at Ecumenical Councils held in the East that the fundamental dogmas of the Christian belief, in the Trinity and the Word of God made flesh in the Virgin Mary were defined'. This Council calls upon all men and especially those 'who make it their aim to further the restoration of the full communion which is desired between the Eastern Churches and the Catholic Church . . . to give due consideration to the special character of the relations which existed between them and Rome before the separation'. Since the Orthodox Churches 'are in possession of true sacraments, notably the priesthood and the Eucharist in virtue of the apostolic succession', some sharing in sacred rites is not only possible but advisable. In short the problem is seen in terms of reuniting, through the decisions of their ecclesiastical authorities, two parts of what is essentially a single whole, but without any suggestion of absorption or assimilation. The Council hopes that 'with the removal of the wall dividing the Western from the Eastern Church, one single building will, at long last, come into existence, firmly based on its cornerstone, Jesus Christ, who will make them both one'.

Striking gestures of friendship which would have been inconceivable even ten years ago have taken been in the direction of the desired reunion. During the Council itself Pope Paul VI made a dramatic visit to the Holy Places, Jerusalem, Bethlehem and Nazareth, to provide an occasion for what proved to be a most cordial meeting with the Ecumenical Patriarch Athenagoras. He followed this after the Council with an official visit to the Patriarch at Istanbul, and Athenagoras in turn came to Rome and was welcomed in St. Peter's, where he laid nine red roses at the Confessio, above the tomb of the Apostle, one for each century of the unhappy division between the Churches of Rome and Constantinople now, it was hoped, being brought to an end. A mutual abrogation of the excommunications which each had made against the other in the 11th century sealed the compact. In June 1970 the Armenian Catholicos followed the Patriarch Athenagoras in a similar conciliatory visit to the Pope. Meanwhile, as we have seen, clerical discussions between Anglicans and Roman Catholics have been progressing and Pope Paul received an official visit from the Archbishop of Canterbury, whom he welcomed at a ceremony in the Sistine Chapel, joining with him in a service of prayer in St. Paul-without-the-Walls before he returned to England.

It would be churlish indeed not to recognise the fraternal charity and goodwill underlying these historic events or to belittle the enthusiasm of the Secretariat for Promoting Christian Unity, now directed by the enthusiastic Cardinal Willebrandts after the death of the much beloved Cardinal Bea, its first head. When, however, we observe how the movement is working out in practice the picture is not so reassuring. Relations with the Eastern Churches have indeed no particular effect upon the internal difficulties of the Catholic Church which we are studying in this book, though they have no doubt a certain impact upon the Oriental Catholic Churches, Melchite, Maronite and others living cheek-by-jowl with Orthodox and other non-Catholic Churches in the Levant. But it is worth remembering that there is scarcely any ecclesiastical unity between the Orthodox. Despite the great historic memories of the Ecumenical Patriarchate, the writ of the Phanar nowadays does not really run beyond the Greeks of Istanbul. The Patriarch himself and his diminished court of metropolitans and other ecclesiastics are all obliged to be Turkish subjects and are the object of many vexatious restrictions. All of the Churches in communion with him are not only particular episcopal churches in the canonical sense. All of them, except the emigré communities in Western Europe and America, are autocephalous national bodies wholly controlled by and committed to the policies of their governments, one non-Communist, namely the Greek, and all the rest Communist. These are allowed to function only as accidental assets to the national foreign policies of civil authorities committed to atheism and world revolution. Some indeed, most of all the Russian, have suffered real persecution but have also been internally weakened and compromised by years of hostile interference. And the Patriarchate of Moscow itself has been guilty of the crudest tyranny in the process of crushing what was the largest of the Catholic Eastern Churches, namely the Ruthenian Uniate Church of the former Polish Ukraine, only one of whose Bishops has escaped death in prison. There is an element of hypocrisy, therefore, in the fulsome flattery meted out to the Eastern Churches in general by the Vatican Council. Nor is there much to admire in the standards of the priesthood or its pastoral record in Greece and the Balkans. Those acquainted with the political realities cannot but be sceptical of the prospects of genuine reunion or even of the good which would result from it.

# Chapter 12

# The ecumenical movement in the West

The practical difficulties of reunion in the West, that is between the Roman Catholic Church and the churches and other communities which owe their origin to the Protestant Reformation, are of a different order. It is not so much a question of governmental control of national churches, though of course the Scandinavian Lutheran Churches are state institutions, with all the inconveniences which this involves, and the Church of England, the old core of the Anglican Church, is formally, though now less rigidly attached to the state. The main difficulty is that Protestant Christianity is based upon the principle of private judgment; there is therefore, despite the ecclesiastical framework and official formularies, no real assurance of unity of belief among Church members. Also, moral standards being more a matter of social convention than of doctrine, it is difficult to discover just where any of these churches stand on such questions, for instance, as divorce, sexual relations outside marriage, abortion and euthanasia. This is not to say that among individual Catholics there are not serious erosions of the moral doctrine and discipline of their Church, as we have seen; yet, for all that there are definite standards, safeguarded by the papal magisterium, which the great majority recognises and which prevail so far as any ecumenical relations with other bodies are concerned.

In this field, as in that of revealed religion and in that of worship, the Church of England practises a wide comprehensiveness. It includes people who hold the most divergent views on the moral issues mentioned above, and attitudes upon historic Christianity which range from complete acceptance of the divinity of Christ, the Virgin Birth, the Resurrection and the miracles of Our Lord to humanist scepticism on all such points. The minority who are active members of their parishes are often admirable Christians, union with whom could only be a joy to Roman Catholics who share the will to realise the prayer of Christ. Yet the majority, if truth be told, never darken a church door except for a wedding or a funeral. The same is certainly true, after Confirmation, of the Lutheran populations of the Scandinavian countries. The standard of belief and church attendance is certainly higher among the reformed churches of North America, including the Episcopal Church, and among Western European Calvinists.

The fact remains, however, that it is very doubtful how far church dignitaries involved in ecumenical discussions with Roman Catholic representatives can really speak on behalf of their church members. So far, because of divergent views sincerely held, it has not been found possible in the United Kingdom to secure a sufficient majority in favour of reunion between the Church of England and the Methodists, the latest body to leave it and the closest to it in faith and practice. And, since Anglican-Roman Catholic negotiations inevitably involve in a more acute form the validity of episcopal consecration and ordination, the principle of the papal primacy and the nature of the Eucharist, it would seem even more difficult to secure genuine and lasting acceptance by a representative collection of clergy and laity of any ecumenical formula which may be devised. Though the old anti-Catholic hatred has almost entirely abated, so much so that the frenzies of the Revd. Ian Paisley and his followers are universally condemned outside Ulster, there are a number of admirable Church of England clergymen (like my forebears on both sides of the family) who have never had the slightest intention or desire to be ordained Catholic priests and who, like an even greater proportion of laymen, have a horror of being 'dictated to' in matters of religious belief. The notion of a national English, rather than a supranational, church is still very real, and not only in the ranks of the 'Establishment'.

These elements have to be set against the group who have been fired by the generous initiative of John XXIII and his successor, to the extent of a willingness to set aside existing habits and prejudices, and the minority of Anglican clergy who have been going so far as to use the Roman missal. The general bonhomie exemplified by the Pope embracing Dr. Ramsay in the Sistine Chapel, or the Archbishop preaching in Westminster Cathedral, or Cardinal Heenan preaching in St. Paul's Cathedral, is a striking novelty which it is easy to applaud. It is a very different matter to determine on whose behalf the higher Anglican clergy could really speak if it came to a deal with Rome. I am not arguing here that any one school of thought is right or wrong, but simply that there is, by the nature of the case, an immense diversity of attitudes, beliefs – and non-beliefs – among the Church of England people of our acquaintance, which is not apparent from the official clerical structure of an episcopal church. It is this which makes reunion between such a body and a unitary religious authority and community, which the Roman Church still is, so difficult to envisage. This is not to say that work of immense value in removing misunderstanding cannot be accomplished by clerical representatives of churches, who really know where they stand and have a minimum of internal divisions, as seems to be the case in the remarkable ecumenical dialogue in the Irish Republic between leading Jesuits and the Anglican Church of Ireland. At the popular level there is a sense of fellowship in singing well-known hymns together – hymns have been called the English religion. The 'Old Hundredth' makes a splendid start for Mass.

However we view it, corporate reunion would be a hollow thing unless it commanded the willing and intelligent assent of the individual persons concerned; assent not merely to the proposition that a united Christian Church is desirable, but assent to definite articles of faith, including those basic tenets of Catholicism, recently affirmed by Pope and Council, which the Roman ecumenist, however tempted he may be to concession and compromise, can hardly throw away without destroying the whole value of the desired union. It is indeed difficult to conceive how in these circumstances the decision to enter or not to enter into full communion with the Catholic Church can ever be anything but a personal one, as it has always been in the past. Ingenious attempts to explain away Leo XIII's ruling against the validity of Anglican orders by discovering an occasional ordination by an Old Catholic bishop during the last century – though this does not touch the real difficulty about the form of the Church of England ordinal – or speculations about the possibility of a Uniate Anglican Church, in which for instance Bishop Butler engages, do not touch the true difficulty, which is the real content of belief, and belief by individual souls.

This opinion is particularly strong, of course, among the many thousands of Catholic converts and among priests who have experience in instructing persons who contemplate joining the Roman Catholic Church, whether on the occasion of marriage or otherwise. It is the main reason for the distrust of the ecumenical programme, to which I allude above, among so many of the Catholic laity, who live and move and have their being among non-Catholic relations, friends and colleagues. Consequently the tendency of ecumenical priests to rush into joint Catholic-Protestant services and manifestations even to the extent of attending Communion services, popular in Holland to the point of throwing almost all distinctive Catholic beliefs to the winds, causes the greatest confusion and disturbance among many English Catholics, and adds to the disarray resulting from the liturgical revolution, the new theology and the anti-papal movement described earlier in this book.

There has also been evidence, in Britain as well as in the United States, of the obstacle created among good Protestants to any possible Christian reunion, not by the traditional tenets about, for instance, the apostolic structure of the Church, the Papacy, the place of Mary in the economy of salvation, the Sacrifice of the Mass, or the moral law itself, but by the tendency of the new Catholic theologians and avant-garde priests to explain away all these things in the Teilhardian sense and to reduce religion to a form of modernist humanism. A Methodist Minister, accustomed to several years of friendly meetings with the local Anglican Rector and the Catholic priest, recently said to his Catholic colleague. 'We always felt, Father, that we knew what you and the Roman Church stood for in the matter of faith and morality. Now we are in the dark'. The solid belief of the Evangelical in the historic truth of the birth, death and resurrection of Jesus Christ, the miracles of the New Testament and the whole doctrine of the Redemption, is as profoundly shocked, as is that of the traditional Catholic, by the antics of the Catholic progressives. And though, notably in the post-Protestant countries, there has been a massive drift towards sexual licence, described as the 'permissive society', there remain good Christian families, among the Free Churches especially, who strongly uphold the sanctity of marriage. While therefore to all appearance it is the progressive, innovating wing of the Roman Catholic Church which is the most forward and vocal in promoting joint ecumenical activities, there is reason to hold that it is itself the great impediment to the real religious unity which, though slow and difficult to realize, is certainly not ultimately unattainable among sincere, believing Christians, Protestant and Catholic, in the Western world. It becomes an even more formidable impediment when political dissension is introduced through the growing involvement of the Catholic Left in the Marxist policies and objectives which we study in the next chapter. A Presbyterian writer, Mr. W. Henry MacFarland makes a cogent observation on this subject in an article in *The American Mercury*,

'Revolutionary changes in its centuries-long teaching

have moved Rome closer and closer, not to traditional Protestantism as many Catholic laymen suppose, but to the humanistic neo-paganism of the National and World Council of Churches. And, coincidental with this "de-christianisation of Christianity" which is working to syncretise the tenets of Protestantism and Catholicism in what amounts to a new "gospel", there has come from the Kremlin what to many appears to be a reciprocatory "softening" in the classical Marxist hatred of and for religion'.

# Chapter 13
## Some political Consequences

**Humanism, the common denominator**

At the youthful level, ecumenism, where it operates, inevitably involves doctrinal indifference – as in the United States, where numbers of young people have come to believe that it does not matter much which place of worship one attends, Catholic or Protestant church, or synagogue, even if one feels a weekly obligation to worship at all. More frequently in Britain there is the inclination not to trouble about religious belief or practice, but to concentrate upon joint humanitarian activities, such as long walks to raise money for *Oxfam* or *Shelter*, or to help various organisations operating to relieve 'world poverty'. One finds a 'wide field for joint witness in social and welfare work' recommended to students in the Ecumenical Directory which I have already quoted, and the massive relief of suffering accomplished by the combined efforts of 'Caritas' and the World Council of Churches in the Nigerian Civil War shows how much can be done by Christian cooperation. It is certainly an admirable development to encourage unselfish work for the developing nations, so long as the money collected really attains useful social and economic ends. But the more this becomes regarded as the *normal* form of Christian activity, the more one senses the idea that the practical religion of the future is purely and simply humanism. Where does God, where does sanctity, where does the supernatural or the sacramental life, come into this? Nowhere. The result is a kind of common denominator of social cooperation as a substitute for faith, which, if it goes on long enough, completely distorts the sense of values upon which Catholic Christianity rests. If one can put aside, for practical purposes, the question of what to believe, as a matter of secondary importance, the danger is that the earnest dialogue of theologians promoted by the Ecumenical Decree of the Vatican Council will end by being left high and dry. It is this kind of humanism which is becoming more and more the meeting ground of Anglicans, Protestants and progressive Catholics in so far as they pursue any common purpose.

Once the habitual field of cooperation has become purely mundane it is extraordinary how quickly it can become political. Ecumenism is a game at which two can play. If from the Catholic side it is a long-term endeavour to draw others into the 'full fellowship' of the Church, it must be remembered that there is another world religion equally convinced that it is right and bound to triumph, namely Marxism, which is entirely and consistently devoted to the world revolution. No sooner is an opportunity offered either for dialogue or practical cooperation with Catholics than it is the obvious and logical gambit of Communism to seize the *main tendue* in order to advance its own cause. We have seen how Communist 'specialists in ecumenism' have emerged in France and Britain, finding their way into the IDOC mechanism. It is easier at the youthful level to turn to advantage the generous impulses for reforming society or freeing the world from want and war; for the 'teenager', unless he has a firm intellectual foundation, is instinctively attracted to radical change, that is to the Left in politics. It is not long therefore before we find young Catholic enthusiasts for the 'third world', endorsing any and every anti-colonial, or anti-imperialist programme, attacking governments for not giving enough money to developing countries, and demonstrating violently against 'apartheid' or for the cause of the negro in America.

It is not long before enthusiasm for peace, for which the Pope constantly appeals, is turned into equally violent demonstrations against the war in Vietnam and Cambodia or rather *one* side in that war, namely the United States. And from the support of such specific causes, laced as they always are with a mixture of self-righteousness and hatred of some class, or race or government, it is a short step to the adoption of the general Leninist thesis that the whole of the established social order must be overthrown. There can, of course, be an extreme case recognised by the Church's teaching on social ethics when revolution against an oppressive government, which has consistently abused its powers, is justified, provided, as the Vatican Council said, that every effort is made to conform to 'the requirements of natural law and the gospel'. These, however, it failed to define: just as it unfortunately shied away from the practical problem of restraining and restricting the use of force in national and international society in favour of the easier and, alas, useless appeal for the abolition of war. The whole object of the Catholic Marxist is to claim Christian justification for violence as a necessary means of social transformation, though Pope Paul VI consistently repudiates recourse to force, and we have Franciscan friars in this country quite untruthfully representing Jesus Christ as a revolutionary in their sermons. We see, from the passionate protests of the Archbishop of Recife, Don Helder Cámara against the repression of political conspiracy in Brazil, how difficult it is in such an inflamed atmosphere to draw the line between violent and non-violent revolution.

## Some fruits of Catholic-Communist dialogue

It would of course be absurd to pretend that most of the young Christians, Catholic and Protestant, who find themselves banded together in humanitarian, social and political movements become committed to the revolutionary extreme. In many cases a sense of humour, religious principle, or the practical needs of educational advance hold them in check. It is nonetheless undeniable that this is the will-o'-the-wisp of the militant student movements which have brought chaos to so many universities of the United States, Japan and the old world. The wild revolutionary propositions of the Père Cardonnel which we have already mentioned played their part in the University rebellion in Paris in 1968; and, to show how far the political revolutionary virus, once it is introduced, can infect the Catholic clergy I reproduce the following deplorable report[41],

> 'The radical priests' organisation "Exchanges and Dialogue", which ended its third national assembly recently in Dijon, has adopted a resolution expressing their "solidarity with the exploited masses" and rejecting the "capitalistic and imperialistic system that is imposed on us". The priests also said that, as the masses struggle against the forces of exploitation in the areas of politics and labour, they must struggle against exploitation in the Church. They accused Church authorities of being 'natural allies of the ruling class' and said that they will work for the "democratisation of the Church".
>
> 'The movement was launched in November 1968, with the publication of a letter demanding that priests be allowed to hold secular jobs, marry and become involved in politics (*The Tablet*, 23 November 1968). It has 800 members, 170 of whom were present at the recent assembly, along with lay representatives of various progressive Catholic movements and the press. According to the answers to a questionnaire distributed during the meeting, 108 of those present had secular jobs, with slightly less than half this number combining a job with pastoral work; 42 were trade unionists; 37 were involved in political organisations; 30 were married and 17 had common law relationships ...

Fr. Julian Walter has sent us the following comment from Paris,

> 'It continues to be the rule in France that priests should not only remain unmarried but also refrain from taking posts in trade unions involving a political commitment, while taking a job is only countenanced in situations where full-time work can serve a pastoral need. The advisability of maintaining this discipline is questioned by many priests. The idea of discussing how priests may

---

[41] *The Tablet*, 9 May 1790.

be "de-clergified", which is why *Echange et Dialogue* was founded, is therefore not without sense. Moreover, Père Jean-Marie Trillard, who was one of the moving spirits behind the movement, is known to be a priest of considerable qualities and experience, particularly in de-Christianised Paris.

'Unfortunately, many of those who joined *Echange et Dialogue* saw it as a way of resolving their own personal tensions rather than as a group concerned with objective pastoral difficulties. They brought into it an element of irresponsibility which has given a false slant to its activities. Those who have taken jobs or enrolled in unions without the authorisation of their bishops, those who have married yet wish to continue to exercise their priesthood, have in fact turned out to be the majority.

'The French episcopate refuses to sanction the movement and the wisdom of their decision not to be represented at Dijon was evident. Although the Bishop of Dijon had authorised a concelebration in a church provided that no married priests took part, those present preferred to hold their concelebration elsewhere. Married priests did in fact take part, and, in order to "de-clergify" the liturgy as much as possible, no vestments were worn and old crockery was used instead of chalice and paten'.

It is evident that Communist 'ecumenical experts' have done their work only too well.


## Anti-colonialism, the new Racialism

This report shows in an extreme form how far dialogue with communism in France has led to the penetration of the minds of priests, closely associated with trade unionists, by the pernicious Marxist doctrine of the inevitable class war. It is no surprise to find those affected by it equally committed to the denial of clerical celibacy and the degradation of the liturgy. One finds this same class consciousness, though in a less vicious degree, in the *Action Catholique Ouvrière* (ACO) and even among the *Jocistes* (*Jeunesse Ouvrière Chrétienne*), who used to be distinguished by their fidelity to the Social Encyclicals of the Popes, both of which groups, for instance, have declined to form part of a proposed diocesan pastoral council in the Archdiocese of Rheims on the ground that they might be outvoted by a majority representing other classes. So much for Catholic unity.

While this entanglement with Marxism may be peculiarly marked in France and some Latin American countries, it seems to be almost an invariable rule that, wherever Catholic organisations or clergy and laity concern themselves with public, and particularly international affairs, they find themselves, sooner or later, adopting the slogans of the Left. This is not surprising. The Communists know what they want and have an unflinching devotion to the political ends of the Soviet or Chinese governments, as the case may be. For a generation they have developed the technique of penetrating the Western 'peace movement' and of exploiting for those ends the divers enthusiasms and prejudices of radicals, humanitarians and social reformers, not to speak of the racial antipathies of Africans and Asians against the Whites. Thus a *set of values* has been created which the progressives (with few distinctions) have come to accept as gospel truths. Among them 'anti-colonialism', which has become the political *credo* of the United Nations, dominated numerically as it is by the Afro-Asians and the Soviet bloc, has come to be regarded as an unquestioned virtue by the innumerable ecumenical do-gooders, for whom concern for the 'Third World' has become a substitute for religion.

In this atmosphere – which is part of our modern world – it was, I suppose, inevitable that the various 'Commissions for Justice and Peace', set up by the Holy See and certain national hierarchies, should have fallen into the trap of accepting the one-sided clichés of the Left. A flagrant example of this may be seen in the following resolutions of the first National Assembly of the Belgian 'Commission for Justice and Peace' which met in Brussels on 7-8 November 1969.

> '(a) That "Justice and Peace" should take a stand on the colonial war which Portugal is waging in Africa; that it should bring pressure to bear on the Government to stop

arms deliveries to Portugal and to influence NATO in this direction; that it should take action on the information media so that the Belgian public may be systematically informed . . .

(b) That the Belgian Bishops, through episcopal meetings on the European scale should intervene with the Portuguese Bishops, so that the latter may recognise their responsibilities in the matter'.

Leaving aside the effrontery of Belgians interfering in the African responsibilities of another country, when they can hardly have forgotten that, on a modest estimate, a million unhappy people lost their lives as a result of their own panic abandonment of the Congo, what is the assumption which forms the basis of such resolutions? The basic assumption is the myth, diffused for a decade by the most unscrupulous and fanatical propaganda, that the Portuguese are conducting a ruthless colonial war to prevent the populations of Angola, Moçambique and Guinea from achieving independence. Highly coloured accounts of the prowess and imaginary conquests of the so-called 'liberation armies', and of the wicked retaliation of the Portuguese (non-existent massacres included), are retailed from time to time in order to sustain this myth on the television and in the Western Press, from *Le Monde* downwards.

## Failure of the 'wars of liberation'

Yet, as every Foreign Office and every responsible journalist outside the Left network knows perfectly well[42], there has never been anything approaching a national rising among the 13 million people of the Portuguese provinces; and, after nine solid years of attacks on these provinces since the first murderous inroads of the Bacongo on the northern Angolan frontier in March 1961, the divers and largely rival 'liberation' movements have had no lasting success, though the Portuguese have had to sustain a considerable military effort to contain them. It is because of this historical failure of the subversive war which they have been waging, despite their

---

[42] e.g. the Africa correspondents of the London *Times* and *Financial Times*.

wishful thinking, that the guerilla leaders and their supporters in the Western World have been making such intensive
efforts to secure popular support, particularly from the
Catholic Left, culminating in their conference in Rome at
the end of June 1970.

Before passing moral judgments it is necessary to realise
why the pan-African offensive against Portuguese Africa
has been such a disastrous military and psychological
failure. There is no need to over-simplify the issue or to
attribute miracles either of virtue or vice to the Portuguese
system of government. Two fundamental reasons have been
discerned by all serious observers. The first is that the Black
*versus* White complex simply does not exist in the Portuguese
territories; consequently the 'major premise' of the anti-
European pan-African argument is missing. The second is
that the raids, coming as they do entirely from foreign bases
in the Congo, Tanzania, Zambia, Conakry or Senegal,
have always been seen by the bulk of the people as a form
of external aggression, whether or not frontier tribesmen
(like the Maconde in northern Moçambique) have been
involved in them. Consequently the counter-insurgency
measures of the Portuguese forces, two-fifths of whom,
Officers, N.C.O's and privates alike, are locally recruited
African soldiery, serving on exactly the same terms as the
Europeans, are in the eyes of the bulk of the population,
Bishops and clergy included, simply an inescapable form of
self-defence, in which any government and people, so placed,
has the right and duty to engage.

These are the bare bones of the case which have no
relation to the incessant anti-Portuguese propaganda endor-
sed by the majority of the United Nations and the myth
which has been sold to the mass media of the Western World.
The fact that it can be swallowed by the 'Justice and Peace
Commission' set up by the Belgian hierarchy, without the
slightest attempt to consult in advance their fellow Catholics
in Portuguese Africa, is as good an example as any of the
disastrous and ridiculous consequences of such amateur

Catholic meddling in international politics and the extent to which it serves the communist cause. Needless to say the question of protesting against the supply of arms to South Africa was raised at the first meeting of the English Catholic 'Commission of Justice and Peace', though fortunately deferred for future discussion. There is a real danger that these well-meaning bodies will simply repeat the ineffective attempts of the League of Nations Union and the United Nations Association to do the government's work for it, arousing in the process the political hostility of many of their fellow-Christians.

# Chapter 14
# A question of international ethics

More serious than the aberrations into which groups of
Catholics have been led in different countries as the result of
their accepting the false set of political values to which I
have referred, is the involvement of the Papacy. For any
apparent encouragement of militant racialism by the Head
of the Church inevitably raises question of moral principle.

Pope Paul VI received the leaders of anti-Portuguese guerilla movements, Amilcar Cabral, Agostino Neto and Mar-
cellino dos Santos, after their conference in Rome, on 1 July
1970, the audience having been requested three months in
advance. If His Holiness, as reported, spoke to them of
general social principles and advised them to pursue their
aims by peaceful means, giving them a copy of his Encyclical
*Populorum Progressio*, it is nonetheless true that his action
was and could only be construed as a form of aid and comfort
to armed insurgency against a friendly people, who, as we
have seen, are doughtily defending themselves. The protest
of the Portuguese Government and the recall of Portugal's
Ambassador to the Vatican were inevitable. An official
reconciliation was effected as the result of a diplomatic
explanation given by the Vatican three days after the event,
a fact which did not deter Mr. dos Santos from claiming in
his report to the Organisation of African Unity at Addis
Ababa on 2 September 1970, that 'the Pope had given
undeniable *de facto* recognition to the fact that the three
movements were the legitimate representatives of the

peoples of Angola, Guinea-Bissau and Moçambique'.[43]
What is much more important than whether or not one
sympathises with the Portuguese is the issue of principle
involved. Does the Pope's friendly gesture to the insurgents
imply, for instance, that he considers his fellow Bishops of
Luso in Angola, or Vila Cabral in Moçambique – to mention two whose dioceses are subject to insurgent raids – are
wrong in supporting the defence of their country? Ought the
Home Guards in their villages to lay down their arms?
These are practical moral questions which arise when a
Pope appears to step down into the political arena, causing
rejoicings on one side of a war, indignation on the other.

## The Papacy and African nationalism

This gesture is unfortunately indicative of a major tendency
in the policy of Pope Paul and his Secretariat of State. The
Holy See has, of course, always been affected by the political
structure of the age. Conservative policies have characterised
both the Holy See itself and the bulk of the national Catholic
communities during the greater part of the modern age,
though the abolition of slavery, a constant papal objective
till its achievement in the middle of the 19th century, and
defence of the workers' rights, since Leo XIII's *Rerum
Novarum* at the end of the century, testified to the obligation
to respect the dignity of human personality both in the
colonial empires and in the industrial states. Christian
democracy, consistently supported by the Papacy after the
fall of Fascism, became the prevailing political theme and
soon dominated not only Italy but most of liberated Europe.
Now, with the collapse of the Empires and the need of
sustaining the vigorous growth of the Church in the en-
franchised African countries and some Asian lands, it is
only natural that the major preoccupation of Papal policy
should have shifted from Europe and North America to the
needs of the so-called developing countries and particularly
to the former dependencies of the Europeans.

---

[43]Reuter and Agence France Presse 9 September 1970.

To respect, help and retain the friendship of the new African states is clearly right and prudent on every ground. The inconvenience of this policy is that decolonisation has become so interwoven with racial passion and revolutionary ideologies, that it is terribly difficult to avoid the accusation of jumping on the anti-colonial band-wagon in such a way as to damage the transcendence and independence of the Papacy, as a conciliatory and pacific power at the service of all nations. Uncritical praise and support of the United Nations which, alas, is very far from being the impartial peacemaker which Christian theory would wish it to be, is the current Vatican policy, and leads to a tendency to endorse the causes dear to its anti-European majority, among them the notion that no Europeans should govern any part of Africa, and that any means to eject them is justified. *Populorum Progressio*, for all its qualifying phrases, was everywhere regarded as an anti-colonial encyclical, assuming that almost all African and Asian countries had rightly achieved independence from European rule and emphasising the duty of the richer industrial countries to assist the development of those backward and underdeveloped, in such a way as to encourage the belief in a guilt-complex underlying this moral obligation of their former rulers. The whole of the Liberal and Socialist elements in the Western World, not to speak of the Communists, have, of course, swung in the same direction and this is not without influence upon the Holy See. So far, though one finds the *Agence Internationale Fides*, the official organ of Catholic missionary activity, repeating the familiar United Nations, Afro-Asian cliché about white 'colonialism' in Southern Africa being a threat to international peace, the Holy See had, until the incident of 1 July 1970, refrained from seeming to give aid and comfort to the unsuccessful 'wars of liberation', to which the majority of the African states are officially committed but, which, having no reasonable prospect of success, cause useless danger and death to many unfortunate Africans.

## The Ethics of Peace and War

The importance of this incident can no doubt be exaggerated, though it was hailed as an event of 'exceptional historic importance' in the Italian press. But it is hard to believe that the consequences could not have been foreseen at the Vatican, and the moral issue is a grave one. Why?

It is the universal assumption of the anti-colonialists and particularly those in the United States who in other respects are often very vocal pacifists, that 'wars of liberation' are always justified, the Ten Commandments notwithstanding; and of course the Communists, who deny the existence of the Moral Law anyway, make the most of them for their own ends. It would be disastrous if the Catholic Church through the acceptance of the clichés of the Left, which as we have seen has already gone dangerously far, accepted this principle. In Pius IX's Syllabus of Errors, now written off by the moderns as a reactionary relic, there is one condemnation which all Christian moralists have hitherto accepted as right, expecially in view of the pretensions of the *Action Française* and the Nazi and Fascist aberrations; it is that of the proposition,

> 'Not only is it not forbidden to violate the most sacred promise or to perform an act which is criminal, sinful and repugnant to the Eternal Law, provided it is done for patriotic motives, but it is right and highly praiseworthy so to act'.

The variant of this error, with which we are now confronted, is that theft, wounding, murder, destruction of property, terrorising of populations and all the other violations of natural law which a war of insurgency involve are justified, indeed virtuous, if committed in the name of race, or of a political theory (viz. self-determination) combined with racial motives.

It is a tragedy that, because of the obsession of the peace lobby to avoid any definition of the traditional 'conditions of just war', the Vatican Council abstained in its Constitution *Gaudium et Spes* from any practical guidance on this subject, though it guardedly admitted the right to self-defence. The whole trend of thought and teaching by responsible moralists of more than a generation is to insist that any use of military force is a great evil and should only be the last resort as a means of defending people, in default of peaceful means, against grave injury from without or within; and the minimum force necessary should be employed. The prime responsibility rests with those who initiate hostilities, not those who resist them. It is not sufficient to have what is, or is believed to be a just cause, which in the case of armed rebellion could only be the existence of a widespread popular reaction to prolonged oppression. There must also be reasonable prospects of success: otherwise the lives not only of the fighters but of many innocent people are uselessly sacrificed. For it must be remembered that the forms of civil society – state, nation or tribe – however organised, have relative, not absolute values. They exist only to serve the moral and material well being of human personality, that is, of invididual men, women and children; and peace and order are the first necessity of every family. It follows that the only form of war which is undoubtedly justified, both in the field of natural morality and of the Christian tradition which has developed it, is the defence of human beings against actual attack or violent molestation, which is exactly what the Portuguese, regardless of colour, believe that they are doing and in fact have done, *contra mundum*, with considerable success.

There is no reason why a war of so-called 'liberation', especially of people which, as Sekou Touré admitted in the case of the African Portuguese, 'do not want to be liberated', should be exempted from these reasonable rules, whatever the ideological enthusiasms of those who launch such wars. The British Foreign Secretary, Lord Hume, as he then was, said in the General Assembly of the United Nations on 1 October 1963,

> 'In Africa the new countries acknowledge the chaos which would follow, if one African country or another were to

try to alter existing frontiers by force of arms. The Addis Ababa conference seemed in this respect to recognise the red light.

'Yet in contemplating what they called wars of liberation to alter the direction of Portuguese colonial policy or to compel South Africa to abandon *apartheid*, they surely fell into the error which they so vigorously denounce in others. For the lesson of the 20th century is the same for African, European or Asian: force can solve nothing, and however strong the political emotions which inspire the desire to employ it, they must be resisted.

'Wars of liberation are nonetheless wars, and it is wars that must be stopped. A nation, it is true, must reserve the right of self-defence in case a neighbour runs amok – that is recognised in the Charter – but example and negotiation, patience and persistence, are the only legitimate means of changing the *status quo*. That is the truth and men everywhere must accept it or all races will die'.

So spoke a Christian statesman; and the government for whom he spoke did its best at that time to prevent the antipathy between leaders of the newly independent African states and Portugal from hardening into the baneful duel which it now is. The British persuaded the Portuguese Foreign Minister, Senhor Nogueira, to meet the African representatives at the United Nations in New York, which he willingly did, since, of course, the Portuguese have no other interest than to live at peace with their neighbours. It was the African nationalists (under intense pressure, it may be said, from the 'American Committee on Africa') who broke off the conversations.

It is a thousand pities that the Holy See should not have used its whole influence in Africa in the interest of this same policy of reconciliation and appeasement, though immediate pastoral advantage rightly influences its attitude to the African states. It is indeed hardly possible to expect African politicians, or indeed most other people, to abate their hostility to the racial discrimination which operates in the South African Republic or Rhodesia, to which the Church itself is inevitably opposed. Yet even here the futility of armed guerrilla attacks to effect the desired change is obvious. With the Portuguese, racial discrimination is not an issue, though criticism of the present system of government is, of course, legitimate; and, as the experience of Malawi shows, it is perfectly possible for the complete respect of African independence to be combined with friendly intercourse and cooperation with Portugal to the mutual advantage of both countries. The question now at issue is not that of a barely possible reconciliation between the small and hitherto unsuccessful bands of insurgents whose leaders the Pope received in July 1970 and any Portuguese Government, since they are now entirely under Communist direction. It is to convince the more responsible African governments of the long-term advantages of peaceful coexistence in the international community and of liberating their national policies from the bondage of hatred.

These however are matters of political judgment compared with the basic issue of international ethics which I have raised. In its implied support of pan-Africanism the Holy See is, of course, only swimming with the tide as, in the context of earlier and different political phases of human society, it has often done before, and not always with desirable results. The Pope himself may be depended upon to save essential religious principles. The inconvenience of the 'leftward lurch' is the encouragement which it gives to those anti-authoritarian elements of the Catholic community which, as we have seen, are already deeply entangled with liberal humanism and Marxism and the damage which it does to the agelong tradition of the Church as the guardian of the Law of Nations.

## A NOTE ON PEACEMAKING IN SOUTHERN AFRICA

I believe that to make peace between Portugal and the independent African states should now be a prime object of Christian statesmanship. The worst that could happen would be the development of the present inconclusive peripheral affrays of insurgency and counter-insurgency, which cost several hundred lives a year, into a major ideological war. This could happen if the short-sighted strategy of the United Nations majority and the Organisation of African Unity succeeded in welding Portugal, Rhodesia and the South African Republic into an effective military alliance (which does not yet exist), while the Communist Powers, which already monopolise – in rivalry – the arming and indoctrination of the anti-Portuguese guerrillas, greatly increased the volume of their reinforcement. Yet the persistent support of their government by the vast majority of Portuguese Africans for more than nine years – of which the increasing number of Africans in the Army, the village home guards and militia (far exceeding the total number of the guerrillas) is the most striking evidence – testifies to the truth of the Portuguese claim to be a non-racial society; and the well-documented educational, economic and social advance of the population of Angola and Mozambique in recent years belies the imaginary charges of 'present humiliation and oppression', which President Nyerere, for one, continues to repeat.

Objectively the war is wholly unnecessary and for that reason immoral. At present there is stalemate. An English priest[44], whose experience is derived from tours in Uganda, Zambia and Tanzania and the propaganda prevalent in those parts, has opined that 'a major war is now going on with almost no prospect of the Portuguese winning it'. The same, of course, could be said of the police in London who can never 'win' the war against crimes of violence; they can only hope to reduce and restrict them. But what is quite clear and is recognised by less emotional and better balanced commentators, such as the authors of the important symposium on Portuguese Africa recently published with the support of the American Center for Strategic and International Studies and the Gulbenkian Foundation[45], is that

---

[44] Rev. Adrian Hastings in *The Tablet*, 22 August 1970.
[45] *Portuguese Africa*, edited by D. M. Abshire and M. A. Samuels. Pall Mall Press 1969.

there is even less military prospect of the insurgents winning it. Now is the time therefore for a determined effort at peace-making, and it is to that end that one could wish to find the Holy See and the World Council of Churches, together with civilised governments, bending all their efforts. Peace-making is always difficult but it is as true of Southern Africa as it was of Northern Africa where St. Augustine wrote it that, *majoris est gloriae ipsa bella occidere verbo quam homines ferro*[46]. The African governments, including those of Congo Kinshasha and the other Francophone states, have nothing to lose and everything to gain, from bringing to an end their futile expenditure on the conflicting liberation movements and reaching a *modus vivendi* with Lisbon, which would make possible the steady development of peaceful interchanges between their peoples and those of the Portuguese provinces. The conclusion of the symposium to which I refer above would be no unworthy aim of Christian diplomacy.

'In the coming crucial decade of educational development, if there can truly be a co-equal assimilation of Portuguese and African values, in a way that appreciates both rich heritages, Angola and Mozambique might take their place in tropical Africa as free and stable societies that would give reality to the Manueline Dream of five centuries ago. They may help show the modern world that the world's oldest continent, unlike some others, is congenial to and mature enough for multi-racial societies, mixing people of diverse colours and ethnic background into one'.

---

'Ep. ad Darium, 229.

# PART SIX

# Conclusions

# Chapter 15
# The Papal position today

We have found much to record, in the development of the
Catholic community during the last eight years, which seems
to give evidence of intellectual derangement and dislocation.
Yet to convinced Catholics like the writer, who could never
doubt the promise of Christ to be always with His Church
till the end of time, there is also much evidence to sustain
their faith. It is to be found chiefly in two phenomena, the
constancy of the Pope and the fidelity of the majority of the
Catholic people.

## The Papal Position today

Consider first the courage and confidence of the Pope
himself. Faced with the humanly impossible task of carrying
out the wishes of a General Council which, one is bound to
conclude, attempted to do too much and so enormously
widened the scope of debate and controversy, Paul VI,
though himself an introvert by nature, has never wavered
for a moment in discharging the unique mandate of Peter
to teach, to rule and to confirm. The Catholic Church would
certainly not survive without this (as we believe) divinely
instituted authority which is the principle of its unity – a
fact which the Church's enemies are the first to realise.
The apparent down-grading of the Papacy, in fact if not in
theory was, as we have seen, the most serious effect of the
Council, through the emphasis given to the power of other
bishops forming with him a collectivity, or college as it is
called, sharing authority. Yet the definition by the First

Vatican Council of the Pope's infallibility and his right to make irrevocable decisions was in fact reaffirmed by the Second; and, despite the campaign which we have described in Part 4, to extend the so-called 'principle of collegiality' to correspond with democracy and to transform the Pope into a constitutional sovereign, Paul VI, in his Encyclicals, his *Credo* and his frequent discourses, has shown that he means to uphold and exercise his unique power and authority as the Vicar of Christ.

Though it causes the modernists to foam at the mouth, this is exactly how loyal Catholics understand his position and expect him to act. For, as one of their most articulate representatives since the end of the Council has expressed it,

> 'The power and authority does not come to him upwards from below, nor from the consent of the Church. It devolves upon him through his office from above, and is the apex of the priestly office at its point of first adhesion into the personal Priesthood of Jesus Christ, before the descent of powers, through order, throughout the body social, which is the Church. Through the fulness of Peter then descends within the People of God the fulness of the magisterium of Our Lord; the body of the apostolic college is a body indeed, but, as every body, it is integrated as through a head, and this head of the visible and corporate body of the Church, in the normal person and natural manner of men, is the successor of Peter'.[47]

Such a statement, intransigent as it may seem, has a truer ring in the ears of the ordinary Catholic than the notion of the Pope as simply *primus inter pares* which the advocates of the 'Conciliar Church' have been propagating as a step to corporate reunion.

Yet, while the Pope remains true to this, his unique post of power and service, there is no vestige in him of the personal arrogance, which is the caricature of the Orangeman. Contrary to the extravagant accusations of the post-Conciliar democrats, he has taken the Council's *Constitution on the Church* seriously and has gone to great lengths – too far, some think – to make collegial consultation with the national

---

[47] Edward Holloway, *Catholicism, a new synthesis*. A Keyway Publication 1969.

hierarchies the normal mode of operation. In short, his way of coping with the centrifugal consequences of the Constitution has not been to oppose a rigid resistance to them, but rather to go along with them as far as possible without relinquishing his ultimate authority. Recently, for instance the Congregation of Divine Worship published the result of an enquiry sent to every bishop in the world on the delicate question of giving Holy Communion either into the mouth or the hand of the recipient, showing that the Pope's decision to confirm the former and traditional practice was the result of more than two-thirds of the Bishops replying in favour of it. Cardinal Alfrink, the Dutch Primate, in an allocation[48] which surprised those who feared – or hoped – that the rebellious spirit of his pastoral council on the celibacy issue would lead to schism – showed how firmly rooted, even in the Netherlands, is faith in the Roman primacy. The occasion was a Mass celebrated at the Hague to commemorate the election of Paul VI and the centenary of the First Vatican Council. He said,

> 'The Catholic conscience of our time cannot isolate the first Vatican Council from the second. The two Councils together are the expression of the authentic faith of the Church, and this faith gives the Bishop of Rome a unique place. In the tradition of the Church that solemn declaration of Our Lord and that promise which is full of hope for all time – "Thou art Peter and upon this rock I will build my Church" – constitutes the *magna carta* of the primacy of him who, because he is Bishop of Rome, is the successor of the first of the apostles'.

And in a tribute to the work of Paul VI, he continued,

> 'He has wholeheartedly collaborated, both as cardinal and later as pope, in the Second Vatican Council. After the Council, by reforming the Curia and by instituting the Synod of Bishops, he has shown that he intends to govern the Church in the spirit of the two Vatican Councils'.

While it is true that there was some sitting on the fence among the Bishops of the Western World, including the

_____
48 28 June 1970.

English, concerning acceptance of the Pope's teaching on marriage and birth control in the Encyclical *Humanae Vitae*, more recent evidence, and especially the reactions to his letter to his Secretary of State on priestly celibacy, following the Dutch initiative, seem to show that he commands the firm support of the great majority of the Bishops of the world. Cardinal Gracias, Archbishop of Bombay, quoted Mahatma Gandhi's tribute to the unique merit of the Catholic priest's celibacy. The African bishops are solid papalists. It seems also that, despite the intrigues of the anti-papal minority, the Pope's relations with the novel Synod of Bishops and its newly established Secretariat in Rome are developing in such a way as to stabilise in a constitutional form the hitherto *ad hoc* consultations between the members and the head of the episcopate. His creation of a theological commission to work as part of the Sacred Congregation for the Doctrine of the Faith, though the ordinary parish priest and practising Catholic layman, who are content with the basic truths of the Christian revelation and the Church's tradition concerning them, can see no need for such a theoretic exercise, will no doubt neutralise the mischief of the new theology by bringing together the rival pundits and knocking their heads together. In short Pope Paul, though lacking the personal magnetism and sense of humour of his predecessor has, it would seem, maintained intact the essential patrimony of the papacy and its hold upon the loyalty of all but a minority of the episcopate.

His visits to all the Continents, though they have ceased to astonish, are without precedent in the history of the Catholic Church and have certainly given the papacy a new dimension. The millions who have seen and heard him either in the flesh or on television, at Bombay, in the Yankee Stadium at New York, at Fatima, at Medellin in Colombia, or at Kampala in Uganda, like those who will be personally affected by his visit to Manila and Australia, have a more immediate sense of his paternity and his mission as the ambassador of God than they could ever derive from 'the prisoner of the Vatican'. At the same time his direct participation in regional or national conferences of bishops which have been the official purpose of several of these expeditions, is a striking demonstration of papal and episcopal solidarity. All this is undoubtedly an asset for the Catholic cause which must be set in the balance against the forces of dislocation and revolt which we have noticed above and whose danger to the sanity of the Catholic mind we must attempt to assess.

Whether the calling of the Vatican Council was inspired, as John XXIII believed, by the Holy Ghost or whether, as it seems to the uncommitted historian judging by the results, it was an act of monumental imprudence, Paul VI, confronted with its aftermath, has undoubtedly deserved well of his people. I believe that there are two fields only in which his pontificate will fairly incur the criticism of history; the diplomatic and the liturgical, and in both he has been much influenced by advisers not of the first order. As to the first, he has succeeded in the best Catholic tradition in making it clear to the world that he and the Church are the champions of international peace, though his actual attempts at peacemaking, whether in the Far East, the Middle East or Nigeria, have been without effect. What has diminished the credibility of his teaching has been the questionable generalisations which are such an unhappy characteristic of pontifical rhetoric. To assert, for instance, that the existing international organisations – meaning the United Nations – provide the necessary means for the settlement of international disputes – is, alas, to substitute wishful thinking for the ugly truth, namely that the basic division between the Communist and non-Communist powers, of which the paralysis of the Security Council is the consequence, and the anti-European majority of the General Assembly, absolutely preclude any possibility of impartiality at the present time, whatever valuable results of practical cooperation can be, and are, achieved by the Specialised Agencies. The uncritical courting of high officials of the main political and financial institutions of the world organisation in New York seems for instance, to have been the main occupation of Mgr. Benelli, the Sostituto or Permanent Under-secretary of the Secretary of State, on his visit to the United States, though one would think that there were desperately urgent pastoral problems of the Church in that country to which a high papal representative could more profitably give his attention. Then there is the almost obsessive personification of 'the Third World' – a purely journalistic nickname for the majority of African, Latin American and Asian states, all, in fact, different from one another in their political, social and economic circumstances – and the adoption of the equally journalistic cliché invented by the French priest who drafted the Encyclical *Populorum Progressio* that 'Development is the new name for peace' (one would have thought *'Pacem dei munus pulcherrimum'*[49] and *'Pax est tranquillitas ordinis'*[50] were better definitions). Undoubtedly it is most desirable to increase the material well-being of peoples with a low standard of living, by supplementing the normal interdependence of international commerce with aid conceived as a social duty. But where can we find any evidence for such an alarmist statement as the following, which occurs in the Pope's address to the Cardinals on 23 June 1970?

> 'There rises from the Third World a cry for help, trusting expectation is turning into terrible denunciation, which could explode in ungovernable rage, whose consequences could be lethal for peace and true progress'.

The actual dangers to peace known to serious students of international affairs come from very different causes. It is this same preoccupation with 'the Third World', identified with the anti-colonial majority in the United Nations, which seems to have led the Pope into so compromising a position regarding the so-called 'liberation wars' in Africa, to the detriment, unintentional I am sure, of international morality. Too much importance, however, should not be attached to errors of judgment in papal diplomacy,

---

[49] Encyclical of Benedict XV, 1920.
[50] St. Augustine, *De Civitate Dei.*

of which the emotional support of Biafra, to the extent of accusing the winning side in the Nigerian war of genocide, was an unfortunate example. Here there is no claim to infallibility. The only criterion of such political acts or statements is their practical feasibility.

The Pope's action in the field of liturgical reform affects the Catholic world much more acutely and undoubtedly diminished the personal devotion which many good Catholics felt for him. Here his historic responsibility for allowing the destruction of a tradition of worship on which the piety and religious culture of centuries had been based is undeniable; nor do I believe that he would wish to deny it, believing it to be justified by a higher good. We have seen the confusing effects of the changes. Doubtless these will diminish in the course of time as churchgoers get used to the new Mass and learn to make the best of it. Here it can be contended that the Pope really need not have let the drive for change in the liturgical Consilium go so far. For instance, during the Council no one outside the côterie of liturgical innovators expected the Canon, the most sacred part of the Mass, to be changed; and, as permission was extended for the use of the vernacular, the Canon was for a time excluded from translation. The advantage of popular understanding and participation, which I think is now admitted by all, could have been combined with the precious supranational unity which is expressed in a common sacred language by having all the early part of the service – the 'Liturgy of the Word' as it is now called – in the vernacular but retaining Latin for the core of the Eucharistic rite. However, the pressure for change and for 'demystifying' the Mass was allowed to go on unimpeded, and persons who notoriously denied the Real Presence of Christ in the Sacrament, as the Pope himself had once more defined it, continued to be active members of the Consilium. This was surely indefensible. Fortunately the essence of the Eucharist, as preserved in the new rite, survived their endeavours, though their influence is discernible, as we have seen, particularly in the vernacular paraphrases which pass for translations. It is even more evident in their speaking and writing which, because of their participation in the official process of revision, gave an appearance of authority to the liturgical experiments which they encouraged and to a number of catechetical deviations. Cardinal Gut, Prefect of the Congregation for Divine Worship, speaking of such experiments has said[51],

> 'What has sometimes happened is that such priests have imposed their will. These initiatives taken without authorisation could frequently not be stopped, because they were already too widespread. In his great goodness and wisdom, the Holy Father then yielded, often against his will'.

This is really a sorry admission of weakness. It may be kind to such vagrant priests: it is not at all kind to thousands of the faithful who suffer from their vagaries.

Subject to these two criticisms of papal action, which it would be dishonest to omit, the main picture of the last five years is of the earthly Head of the Catholic Church, holding his own against persistent attacks. We have quoted more than one example of his deploring of contemporary errors. Latterly he has been taking a more philosophical view of the post-conciliar perturbation. This, for instance, is how he described it in addressing the Cardinals after the Consistories of 15 December 1969,

> 'Internally and externally the Church has shown, not the placid fervour that the Council gave us to hope for, but in some limited, yet significant sectors, a certain inquietude. The difficult interpretation of the signs of the time wakened in many a new and absorbing study of contingent reality, drawing from it not only wise observations, but in some the mania of novelty, and in others the fear of reform. To a pluralism, sometimes indiscriminate, of ideas and forms, that seems to menace the intimate organic unity proper to the Catholic Church, is added an increasing tendency towards theological research and a more active need for organic community relations. To a decreasing

---

[51] Documentation catholique, 16 November 1969.

fervour in personal religious life is to be contrasted an increasing interest in collective devotion. To a movement towards secularisation that tries to desacralise everything, there may be joined a greater social sense of Christian responsibility'.

Upon which one is tempted to quote Hamlet 'To be or not to be, that is the question'. Yet despite this somewhat Olympic detachment, followed by an appreciation of much that he found consoling in the Church today, the Pope went on to say that the ship of the Church felt the buffeting of the storm characteristic of our time. It brought to his mind the sorrowful words of his predecessor St. Gregory the Great in his letter to Leander, Bishop of Seville[52],

'At one time the waves beat against us, at another from the side the foaming mountains of the sea swell up, at another from the stern the storm pursues us. In the midst of all this with troubled mind I am driven at times to steer into the very heart of the storm, at times, turning the ship aside, to steer away from the menacing waves. I groan'.

'Yes, venerable Brothers, it cannot be denied that there exist in the Church today misfortunes, dangers, needs'.

---

[52]Patrologia Latina 77.497.

# Chapter 16
# The forces of disorder summarized

The principal dangers, which make it not at all unreasonable for observers in the Western World to ask the question to which this book is addressed 'Has the Catholic Church gone mad?', emerge clearly enough from what we have recorded in our chapters on the Conciliar Church campaign, the Democratisation of the Church and the New Theology. It is impossible to believe that the Catholic Church could survive, as the distinctive entity which we know it to be in its history and in its doctrine, if it were turned into a kind of international religious republic with elections, and therefore party contests, at every level from the parish to the remnants of the papacy: for that is really the logical consequence of 'coresponsibility' all round. It might work, of course, if there were no original sin: but in that case there would be no Church anyway. As for the campaign of the new American 'Establishment', it is almost wholly negative. Inspired by the deep-rooted anti-authoritarian spirit bred of that strange combination of Puritanism and the enlightenment of the 18th century which formed the American mind, it is essentially anti-Papal and finds its natural allies in the old seed grounds of Calvinism and Rationalism in Western Europe. By instinct it criticises or opposes all that the Pope teaches by virtue of his unique authority, be it the traditional tenets of the Creed or the moral restraints upon sex; for the sexual obsession is most virulent in the post-Protestant countries. This kind of 'progress' is but the veneer of the old *non serviam*. Meanwhile, and closely associated by a

network of personalities with these movements of democratisation and revolt against authority, the new theology
develops as a means of adapting Christianity to evolution
and modern psychology, undermining in the process belief
in the objective reality of historic Christianity and in the
personal responsibility of the human creature to God. When,
therefore, it is a question of finding a common basis of
cooperation between Catholics infected with these ideas and
non-Catholics, under the banner of ecumenism, it is not
surprising to find that it is no form of supernatural belief but
natural humanism that eventually provides the common
denominator. Despite the good intentions and qualifications
of individuals, this is not, I believe, an unfair assessment of
the forces operating to rot the common mind and will of
the Catholic body.

The strength of those involved in these movements, all
of which claim to be means of carrying forward the general
renewal of religion initiated by the Second Vatican Council
(all that was done and taught before it being relegated to the
scrap heap), lies not in their numbers (which are unascer-
tainable), but in their command of the mass media of
communication in the Western World. We have described
the mechanism of their operation in Chapter 8. It means
that, for six or seven years at least, full publicity and editorial
support have been given – simultaneously as a rule in many
countries – to the views and news which they wish to
propagate whereas any utterances or letters of the Pope
which they do not approve are suppressed, consigned to
back pages or held up to ridicule. How many Catholics in
these countries have heard of, let alone read, his *Credo of the
People of God*, which he particularly intended as a popular
handbook of belief? The same treatment has been meted
out in the controlled press to any important publications or
meetings of Catholic intellectuals who do not conform to the
approved progressive trends. Who for instance, reading the
Catholic press, would know of a congress of some 2,000 people
which has met at Lausanne several years running at Easter

for a stiff discussion of Christian social action based upon Natural Law?

The result of this propaganda over a number of years has been to create in the minds of a vast number of people and particularly young people, priests included, the same kind of acceptance of a supposed progressive high road to the future as the Left Establishment in television and the press has created in the sphere of politics. Indeed the two very often coalesce. Thus there is an instinctive refusal to listen to teaching or argument which upholds traditional doctrine or moral rules, such as the forbidding of contraception. In fact one finds, as in temporal affairs, that the progressive enthusiast often has a closed mind: it is, for instance, impossible to persuade young priests affected by the new theology to read a book which criticises the theories of Teilhard de Chardin. Rational argument has little place in such an atmosphere. The worst effects of this upon the younger generation come from the new catechetical methods, since progressives with such *idées fixes*, like Brother Moran in the United States, have secured control of the principal catechetical institutes and publications. On the ground that the old method of question and answer ('Why did God make you?') is obsolete, a kind of environmental chatter has come in ('Where did Mary buy her groceries, as there were no buses?'), which vaguely introduces a few Biblical events in a contemporary setting, but leaves the child with no clear knowledge of God, of Sin, of Redemption, of the great events of the Birth, Life, Death and Resurrection of Jesus Christ, of the Ten Commandments, or the laws of the Church.

Most serious is not only the decline in the number of vocations to the priesthood and the religious life – added to the notorious defections – but the nature of the training in the seminaries and novitiates. In many of them the introduction of the new ideas, combined with a disastrous relaxation of discipline and dress, have resulted in an atmosphere which is most unpropitious to the production of educated men, firm in their convictions and wholly consecrated to their priestly duties, such as those who have been the real pillars of the Faith in our parishes in recent generations. It is obviously unfair to generalise on this subject, but there is too much evidence of the decline to permit of any optimism concerning the leadership which can be expected of a diminishing clergy during the next decade or two. The real test for Catholicism in the Western World will come when the middle-aged and elderly priests of today, who were trained in a harder school and have lived in a sound pastoral tradition, die or retire. It will be a tremendous task for the Bishops, not just to hold the balance, as they have been doing, between divers innovating or conservative tendencies and steer through a maze of committees and councils, but to restore a high standard of basic teaching and practice.

# Chapter 17

# The issue in perspective

While, humanly speaking, the outlook is therefore bleak, it must be remembered that all that I have recorded applies to the affluent societies of North America, Western Europe and Australasia 'where wealth accumulates, and men decay' and to communities of European extraction in Latin America. There are other parts of the world in which the Catholic body is, by all accounts, relatively free from the dissolvent and disruptive influences which we have described.

At the Pan-African Bishops' Symposium held at Kampala in 1969, Cardinal Zoungrana was given a standing ovation for his opening speech in which he said that it was inadvisable for the Church in Europe to foist its pseudo-problems, such as clerical celibacy and the so-called population explosion, on to the African church. Neither was a problem in Africa. Bishop Usanga, Secretary General of the Catholic Secretariat of Nigeria, commenting upon this to a correspondent[53] said,

> 'We insisted at the Kampala conference that it was not celibacy which was the obstacle to plentiful vocations. A much more serious obstacle to our mind was the tendency to relax the discipline in the seminaries, and also the introduction of certain hypotheses – mere hypotheses but taught as if they were defined doctrine. This, of course, leads to confusion of the students, who maybe leave the seminary or hesitate about presenting themselves for the priesthood . . . Discipline in the seminaries should not be relaxed. It was felt very strongly that priests must be

[53]of *Africa*, published by St. Patrick's Missionary Society, Kiltegan, Co. Wicklow, Ireland.

trained to self-denial, sacrifice and service, and that this will not be accomplished by the relaxation of the old-fashioned discipline in the seminaries. African priests brought up in this discipline will continue to persevere in their priestly vocation'.

I end with this quotation for it puts the intellectual pride of the White Man in its place. The Catholic Church has not gone mad. In so far as Catholic minds have gone mad it is *not* a universal phenomenon: it is a European phenomenon, and is the consequence of attempts to adapt and accommodate a religion based upon man's entire dependence on God (a humble and a contrite heart and the fear of the Lord which is the beginning of wisdom), to the conditions of a society in which pride in man's scientific achievement and his supposed social and intellectual emancipation has led to a general impatience with authority at every level and disbelief in the moral law itself. The solidity and sanity of the Church recently established in the far poorer but more naturally God-fearing society of Africa – shared, as we believe it to be, by a large but inarticulate part of the Catholic clergy and people in other continents – is proof that what is trumpeted abroad as progress, whether in the form of loosening ecclesiastical authority and discipline or in modernising faith and morality, is in reality the peculiar product of a decadent European civilisation, which, historically Christian in origin, can no longer claim the name of Christendom. Certainly the immense facilities provided in the world today by instantaneous communications and the mass media of information give to the exponents of political, social and religious notions in the affluent Western world, as they do to the Marxists, a means of reaching the minds of men in every part of the globe, so that, when considering the attacks upon the integrity of the Catholic mind, we have to estimate their effects not only in their countries of origin. But the fact remains that it is chiefly in Western Europe and North America that this disarray has been created, and it is there that the struggle to counteract it must be waged. Important as may be the debates about the distribution of powers in the Church, or regard for human freedom, or the adaptation of doctrine to the scientific and philosophical fashions of the day, or the social order, it is time to recall that these at the best are only means to an end, which is a spiritual end. The first and most important mark of the Church of Christ is holiness. It is a mark which today is much beclouded. Charity and justice indeed are the adjuncts of sanctity, but so, in this boisterous world, are reverence, awe, humility, and quiet in the contemplation of divine mysteries. These, and not the reorganisation of human society are what at its best the Catholic Church has offered to humanity in past centuries, and it is these intangible qualities and virtues which at all costs must be restored and preserved.

# INDEX